*TWAYNE'S WORLD AUTHORS SERIES*

*A Survey of the World's Literature*

Sylvia E. Bowman, Indiana University

GENERAL EDITOR

# CHINA

William R. Schultz, University of Arizona

EDITOR

# Hsiao Hung

*TWAS 386*

Hsiao Hung

# HSIAO HUNG

By HOWARD GOLDBLATT
*San Francisco State University*

TWAYNE PUBLISHERS
A DIVISION OF G. K. HALL & CO., BOSTON

**Library of Congress Cataloging in Publication Data**
Goldblatt, Howard, 1939-
  Hsiao Hung

  (Twayne's world author series; TWAS 386)
  Bibliography: p. 153–58.
  Includes index.
  1. Chang, Nai-ying, 1911–1942.
PL2740.N3Z64      895.1'3'5 [B]      75-30650
ISBN 0-8057-6228-0

Dedicated to my Mother and
To the memory of my Father

# Contents

# About the Author

Howard Goldblatt was born in Long Beach, California, and received his B.A. from California State University at Long Beach in 1961. He spent four of the next seven years in Taiwan as a naval officer and later as a full time student of Chinese. He received his M.A. in Chinese from San Francisco State University in 1970, after which he served as an instructor at the university for one year. He received his Ph.D. from the Department of East Asian Languages and Literatures at Indiana University in 1974, spending his final year as a Fulbright Fellow in Kyoto, Japan. His articles in Chinese and English and translations of modern Chinese literature have appeared in several periodicals, including the *ASPAC Quarterly, Dousou, Renditions,* and the *Chinese PEN Quarterly.* He is presently an assistant professor of foreign languages in the Chinese Program at San Francisco State University.

# Preface

The decade of the 1930's was one of intense activity in China in nearly all fields of human endeavor. Thoughts of war were occupying increasingly large segments of the population of the young republic, whose twenty-year existence had witnessed a spreading but incomplete democratic revolution, a brief return to monarchy, periodic and devastating clashes with and between warlords, the founding of the Chinese Communist Party, and its slow but inexorable growth. In the field of literature these chaotic years witnessed a dramatic shift in direction, one which has been characterized as a change from a literary revolution (of the 1920's) to revolutionary literature. This pronounced shift to the left involved the great majority of nationally known writers, a phenomenon that placed the literary community in the forefront of the revolution and the struggle against Japanese encroachments. As a consequence, the role of writers in the social and political scenes during this period was one of vast importance.

Among the most popular and successful new talents of this period were several writers from Northeast China, whose emergence on the literary scene was largely contemporaneous. Members of this Northeastern Group of Writers (*Tung-pei tso-chia ch'ün*) were highly active literary figures throughout the 1930's and 1940's and in some cases even beyond. One of them, Hsiao Hung, emerged as the group's most interesting figure and quite possibly its most gifted writer; romantically involved with two of her fellow Northeastern writers, she also maintained a friendly and often very close relationship with at least four others. She came into national prominence following the publication of her first novel and remained a well-known and highly acclaimed writer throughout most of the remainder of her career. Though evidently a member of no political party nor an active member of any significant literary organization, she was, nonetheless, a colleague and close personal friend of many important literary figures of her day. And yet Hsiao Hung has suffered an almost total neglect at the hands of Western students of contemporary Chinese literature, even though materials on her, while meager in some respects, outnumber those on the other members of the Northeastern Group of Writers and, for that matter, many of the most prominent literary figures of that period.

As regards the biographical portion of the present study, the goal has been a complete and completely accurate chronicle of Hsiao Hung's life. Inevitably, that goal has not been entirely realized. It is not that too few materials on her exist (though for certain periods that is part of the problem), for a glance at the Bibliography will show that such is not the case in general; rather, the materials all too often contribute totally unsubstantiated information or data that are hopelessly contradictory. The end result has been a chronicle with occasional gaps, large and small, where accurate or definitive information is simply unavailable.

Lamentable as the occasional gaps in the reconstruction of Hsiao Hung's life may be, in respect to her literary works we possess all the data we need: the three novels, numerous short stories and sketches, and several poems and occasional pieces written by her between 1933 and 1941. The format selected for this study is one of examining Hsiao Hung's writings in the context of her life and times so that we can more easily see her remarkable progress as a creative writer and perhaps get some understanding of why any given work failed or succeeded. Inasmuch as her total output is of manageable size, the entire corpus has been examined and discussed, to a degree commensurate with the literary qualities and importance of each piece. One of the unavoidable results of discussing the works as they appeared chronologically has been an occasional interruption in the biography, although it is felt that the net loss in continuity is more than compensated for by the greater understanding of her works such a format affords us.

# *Acknowledgments*

Independent as a work of scholarship may be, it is difficult to imagine any study such as this one reaching completion without any outstanding debts of gratitude. Although it is impossible to thank each and every individual who contributed to this work, several acknowledgments are in order. I am indebted to the Fulbright Commission whose grant made it possible to spend a long uninterrupted period of time on research and writing. My thanks also to those who helped me in the gathering of materials, especially Shizue Matsuda, Indiana University; Professor Maruyama Noboru, Tokyo University; Tatsuma Syosuke and Ichikawa Hiroshi, Tokyo; Wong Chun-tong, Hong Kong; Chou Chin, Taipei; and Raymond Tang, University of California. Many people have kindly read my manuscripts, and I would like to thank especially Professor William Schultz of the University of Arizona and Heather Ion for their many helpful suggestions. I have been particularly fortunate to have the opportunity to interview several of Hsiao Hung's friends: I would like to thank publicly Sun Ling, Ch'en Chi-ying, Sun Kuei-chi, and his wife Chang Yü-lien, in Taiwan; Li Hui-ying, in Hong Kong; and Kaji Wataru, in Japan. Finally, special thanks are due two scholars without whose assistance this work could never have been completed: Professor Takeuchi Minoru of the Center for Humanistic Studies, Kyoto University, and Professor Wu-chi Liu of Indiana University. It is hoped that this study will not prove unworthy of the assistance and guidance it has been my great pleasure to receive.

HOWARD GOLDBLATT

*San Francisco State University*

# Chronology

1911    Born in Hulan County, Heilungkiang Province, Northeast China
1928    Enrolls in Harbin First Municipal Girls' Middle School
1930    Returns to Hulan (summer)
        Flees to Harbin to avoid arranged marriage
1931    Travels with lover to Peking
        Mukden Incident (September 18)
1932    Returns to Harbin alone
        Meets Hsiao Chün (July?)
        Gives birth to daughter
        Begins writing career
1934    Flees Harbin and travels with Hsiao Chün to Tsingtao (May)
        Travels with Hsiao Chün to Shanghai (October-November)
        Meets Lu Hsün (November)
1935    *The Field of Life and Death* published (December)
1936    Travels alone to Japan (summer)
        *Market Street* published (August)
        Lu Hsün dies (October 19)
        *The Bridge* published (November)
        Returns to Shanghai
1937    *On the Oxcart* published (May)
        General war with Japan breaks out (July 7)
        Travels to Wuhan with Hsiao Chün (August-September)
        Meets Tuan-mu Hung-liang
1938    Travels to Lin-fen (Shensi) (January)
        Leaves Hsiao Chün and becomes common-law wife of Tuan-mu Hung-liang (February)
        Returns to Wuhan via Sian with Tuan-mu Hung-liang (April)
        Travels to Chungking (September)

1940    Flees to Hong Kong with Tuan-mu Hung-liang
         *Ma Po-lo* published (December?)
1941    Enters Queen Mary's Hospital
         Japanese attack Hong Kong (December 8)
1942    Operated on for suspected throat tumor (January 13)
         Dies of throat infection (January 22, 11:00 A.M.)
         Cremated and buried near Repulse Bay (January 24)
         *Tales of Hulan River* published posthumously
1946    *A Cry in the Wilderness* published posthumously
1957    Ash remains moved to Canton (August 3)
1958    *Selected Works of Hsiao Hung* published (December)

### CHAPTER 1

# Hulan River:
# "Perpetual Longing and Pursuit"

TO the north of China proper, situated between the Great Khingan Mountains in easternmost Mongolia, Siberia to the north and east, and the Yellow Sea and Korean Peninsula to the south lies the Great Manchurian Plain. Although best known to the West as Manchuria, this area is normally referred to by the Chinese as the Three Eastern Provinces (Heilungkiang, Kirin, and Liaoning), or simply as the Northeast (Tung-pei).

At the turn of the twentieth century the population of the entire area probably numbered no more than thirty million, a high percentage of whom were Chinese who had emigrated there from south of the Great Wall in the declining years of the Manchu (Ch'ing) Dynasty. Owing to its fertile plains and highly productive soil, the principal wealth of Manchuria lies in its agricultural output. Heilungkiang, the northernmost province, is "the land of the greatest plains and the greatest rivers, and of mountain ranges almost unpenetrated."[1] Its capital city, Harbin, is located in the south of the province on the Sungari River (one of the two major rivers of the area, the other being the Amur), which flows north through Kirin and then east past Harbin, gradually heading in a more northerly direction where it waters the Amur Valley.

During the early decades of the twentieth century, Harbin, one of the great cities of Manchuria, was populated mainly by immigrants, Chinese and Russian. It was, in fact, the city in which the majority of Russian exiles from the October Revolution who had come to China were concentrated. About twenty miles north and slightly west of Harbin lies the county of Hulan, named after the Hulan River, a small tributary of the Sungari which runs through it. On the northern bank of the Hulan River and a few miles west of the spot where it branches off from the Sungari, is the town of Hulan.[2] Like so many towns which are located in the heart of an agricultural district, it consisted of little more than marketplaces where the peasants sold their excess produce, some shops which catered to their nonagricultural needs, schools, and residential areas. Its physical makeup and general atmosphere during the early 1900's have been described in simple but picturesque terms in Hsiao Hung's novel *Hu-lan-ho chuan (Tales of Hulan River):*

Hulan River . . . is not a very prosperous town at all. It has only two major streets, one running north and south and one running east and west, but the best known place in town is the crossroads, for it is the nucleus of the whole town. At the crossroads there is a jewelry store, a fabric shop, a dry goods store, a teashop, a pharmacy, and the office of a foreign dentist. Above this dentist's door there hangs a large signboard on which is painted an oversized row of teeth, each one almost as large as a rice-measuring cup. The advertisement is hopelessly out of place in this small town, and the people who look at it can't figure out just what it represents. The reason is that neither the dry goods store nor the fabric shop displays any kind of advertisement; above the door of the dry goods store, for example, only the word "salt" is written, and hanging above the door of the fabric shop are two cloth curtains which look as though they have been there since antiquity. . . .

In addition to the crossroads there are two other streets, one called Road Two East and the other called Road Two West. Both streets run from north to south, probably for five or six *li*. There is nothing much on these two roads worth noting—a few temples, several stands where flat cakes are sold, and a number of grain storehouses . . . .

On Road Two East there are also two schools, one at the southern end and one at the northern end. They are both located in temples—one in the Dragon King Temple and the other in the Temple of the Patriarch—and both are primary schools.

The school located in the Dragon King Temple is for the study of raising silkworms and is called the Agricultural School. The one in the Temple of the Patriarch is just a regular primary school with one advanced section added, and so is called the Higher Elementary School.

Although the names used for these two schools vary, in fact there is no real difference between them. It's just that in the one they call the Agricultural School, when autumn arrives the silkworms are fried in oil, and the teachers enjoy several sumptuous meals.[3]

By all indications, then, Hulan was a quiet and rather backward town peopled by conservative and superstitious peasants, craftsmen, shop owners, a few lettered individuals who served as teachers, and the ever-present gentry. And it was to one of the latter families that Hsiao Hung was born in 1911, the year in which the Manchu Dynasty was overthrown.[4] The first child of the well-to-do Chang family, whose ancestors had emigrated from the Shantung Peninsula, she was given the name Nai-ying.

Hsiao Hung's father was the head of the family and the master of a large compound located in the outskirts of town.[5] Hsiao Hung does not mince words where her father is concerned; she writes:

> My father often gave up his humanity over his own covetousness. His relationships with servants, or with his own children, as well as with my grandfather were all characterized by his stinginess, aloofness, and even hard-heartedness.
>
> Once, over a rent payment due on a house, my father took possession of a tenant's entire team of horses and his wagon. The tenant's family wept, pleaded, and prostrated themselves at the feet of my grandfather, who then unharnessed two tawny horses from the wagon and gave them back to them.
>
> My father quarrelled with my grandfather all night long over those two horses. "Two horses to us mean nothing, but to a poor man those two horses mean his very existence," my grandfather said, but my father continued quarrelling with him.
>
> When I was nine my mother died. My father changed even more; when someone on occasion broke a glass, he shouted and carried on until the person shook in his boots. Afterwards it seemed as though my father's glance could take in everything around him, and at such times, whenever I passed by him I felt as though my body were covered with thorns. He would cast an oblique glance at me, and that arrogant look of his would shift from the bridge of his nose, down past the corner of his mouth, and continue moving down.
>
> So at dusk during snowstorms I stayed near the heater and by my grandfather, where I listened to him reading poetry and watched his slightly reddened lips as he read the poems.
>
> Whenever my father beat me, I went to my grandfather's room and stared out the window from dusk to late into the night.[6]

The mother whom Hsiao Hung lost when she was nine fared no better in her eyes. In "The Family Outsider," a long story written along the lines of *Tales of Hulan River*, the author admits that she was afraid of her mother, who often hit and even threw stones at her.[7] Elsewhere she has written laconically that her mother was a woman of "mean words and nasty looks."[8] Hsiao Hung's Chinese biographer, Lo Pin-chi, writes that her father later remarried;[9] evidently her situation did not noticeably improve, for, according to a later friend, she was also treated badly by her stepmother.[10] When Hsiao Hung was three or four years old, a son was born to the family;[11] although he was evidently devoted to his elder sister, Hsiao Hung was never able to reciprocate the affection this heir to the family fortunes and recipient of their father's love had for her.[12] Hsiao Hung's father, a strict disciplinarian, seemingly kept hidden whatever love he had for his eldest child, especially after the birth of his son. Also, the multifarious affairs of a landlord, coupled with the overseeing of the family compound, must have kept him very busy indeed, too busy to spend much time with his children.

The central figure in Hsiao Hung's youth was her grandfather, about whom she has written with great tenderness and love, both in *Tales of Hulan River* and in some of her prose sketches. The bond she felt for this humane and kindly man influenced her throughout her life, and his memory was the source of many of the rare moments of happiness in her final years. Although he died when she was still in her early twenties, she never forgot his love for her and her days at his side:

Granddad wasn't any good at financial matters, and all the household affairs were handled by my grandmother. Granddad simply passed his days relaxing to his heart's content, and I felt it was a good thing I had grown up—I was three—otherwise, how lonely Granddad would have been. I could walk . . . I could run. When I was too tired to walk Granddad carried me, and then when I felt like walking again he pulled me along. Day in and day out, inside or out of doors, I never left his side; for the most part, Granddad was in the rear garden, and so that's where I was too.[13]

If Hsiao Hung's grandfather was the most important person in her early life, the garden was the most important place. Not only did it provide the ideal spot in which to escape the oppressive atmosphere of the house, but it also was the site of her earliest and most satisfying contact with nature. The sensitivity for nature she derived from this garden sparked a youthful desire in her to become a painter, and when she later turned to writing instead, it provided the inspiration for some of her most memorable scenic passages. Besides playing in her garden, whether admiring its plants and flowers or happily chasing the many insects there, she delighted in lying down in the soft grass to sleep, and it was there that she often brooded over her treatment by her elders.

Prominent among those members of the family whom she did not like was her grandmother. Unwilling to tolerate the playful exuberances of her young granddaughter, this ailing and domineering woman is remembered by Hsiao Hung as the one who "used a needle to prick [my] fingers."[14] But it was the old woman's attitude toward Hsiao Hung's beloved grandfather that was the real cause of the enmity the young girl felt towards her:

All day long Granddad was idle, as Grandmother was unwilling to give him any jobs to do. There was just one thing: her coffin, which was on the floor, had a set of pewter ornaments and these Granddad regularly polished. I'm not sure if he was given this assignment by her, or if it was something he undertook to do on his own. But whenever he began to polish them, I became unhappy, partly because this meant he couldn't take me out to play in the rear garden, and also because he would often be yelled at; Grandmother would scold him for being lazy and scold him for not doing a good job of polishing. And whenever she began to scold him, somehow or other even I got yelled at.[15]

Hsiao Hung was six years old when her grandmother died, and this event plus the long illness which preceded it caused mixed emotions on her part. Certainly she experienced no feelings of loss (her tender age and general dislike of the old woman precluded such a reaction), but during this period her grandfather was increasingly occupied with caring for his wife and later with her funeral, and Hsiao Hung thus experienced great loneliness. Some good must have been gained from the period of her grandmother's passing, as there was a constant influx of family members, including several young cousins with whom Hsiao Hung enjoyed many carefree days. It was also during the period just after her grandmother's death that Hsiao Hung left the family compound for the first time, travelling in company with some of her cousins to the riverbank less than one *li* from her home. On the way to and from the spot she discovered sights that her garden neither had nor could equal in terms of grandeur and fascination and realized that the world possessed a great many things she had never seen before. In her own words: "Therefore Grandmother died, while I actually gained in wisdom."[16]

The family compound where Hsiao Hung lived included more than thirty rooms, although she and her family occupied only the main house, which consisted of five rooms—two for her grandparents, two for her father and mother and the children, plus a kitchen. Additionally, there were two small and dark storage rooms attached to the rear of the house in which the relics of several generations of the Chang family were kept. During inclement weather Hsiao Hung spent long hours in the storerooms carefully investigating—and occasionally breaking—the myriad of long-forgotten objects that she found there. The remaining buildings in the compound were either used by the family to store grain (" . . . There was little grain, but hordes of rats."), or were rented out, either to a family of pig-raisers or to a noodle-maker. The people who lived in the compound were a varied lot, and Hsiao Hung was often treated to exciting spectacles, both tragic and humorous.

As all members of the gentry are expected to receive an education, Hsiao Hung eventually had to forego some of her carefree outings in the garden and begin her lessons. The responsibility for making a literate person of her evidently was entrusted to her grandfather, for in her childhood reminiscences she recalls her introduction to classical poetry via his readings of the *Ch'ien-chia shih*, a traditional collection of perennial favorites. Like most Chinese children, she felt attracted to particular poems, not because of their content (in fact, one poem she especially liked was ruined for her once its meaning was made clear), but because of their sound and imagery; she was particularly fond of nature poems. When she reached school age she entered one of the local primary schools, though we do not know whether it was the Higher Elementary School or the Agricultural School.[17]

As must be evident by now, the account of Hsiao Hung's life in the town of Hulan given above covers only the period of perhaps her first ten years. What her teens were like (she first left Hulan at about the age of seventeen or eighteen) must for now remain unanswered, since she neither wrote about those years nor, evidently, did any of the friends whom she might have taken into her confidence. And yet, for our purposes, the most important aspects of her life in the Chang compound are already apparent. It is difficult to gauge the emotional impact the attitudes of her mother (or stepmother) and grandmother had upon her, but her reactions to the disinterested, avaricious, mean, and perhaps cruel behavior of her father were bitter anger and a profound sense of injustice. At a chance meeting with her brother in the city of Harbin during one of her most trying periods, she responded to his entreaties to return home by saying angrily: "I cannot go back to that kind of home. I'm not willing to be supported by a father who stands at the opposite pole from me."[18] Her relationship with her father unquestionably constituted the genesis of much of the personal bitterness she later manifested in her writings; moreover, it undoubtedly also helped shape her distaste for such remnants of traditional Chinese society as male supremacy and the arranged marriage system.

As we have already noted, the effect Hsiao Hung's grandfather had on her was very different. A close reading of the relevant chapters of *Tales of Hulan River* and some of her autobiographical sketches makes clear that not only did he supply his granddaughter with most of the love she received in her youth, but he also nurtured in her a strong sense of humanity and a love for nature and beauty. As she later remembered it, he was the only person in the family to speak out against the social injustices which often puzzled and usually horrified her. She later wrote:

Granddad often placed his two wrinkled hands on my shoulders, then on my head, and my ears rang with sounds of:

"Hurry and grow up! It will be fine once you have grown up."

The year I reached the age of twenty I fled from the home of my father, and ever since I have lived the life of a drifter.

I've "grown up," all right, but things are not "fine."

But I learned from my grandfather that besides coldness and hatred, life also includes warmth and love.

And so, for me there is a perpetual longing and pursuit to find this warmth and love.[19]

Two other influential forces operated on Hsiao Hung in the town of Hulan: the lives of the peasants and her own loneliness. Although a member of the landed class, she evidently spent a good deal of her time in direct contact with the peasants living in and around Hulan. The impressions she gained of peasant life were lasting ones. Inasmuch as members of the peasantry were to play leading roles in two of her most important works, her relations with and knowledge of the peasantry will be explored later.

Loneliness, too, was to remain with her—to plague her, as it were—throughout her life. Hers was the loneliness of a child raised in a family where love was in short supply and in an environment where there were few playmates. If her later life is any indication, we must conclude that she was an exceptionally sensitive child, and the sense of loneliness that literally permeates the pages of her childhood reminiscences certainly had a marked effect on her.

### CHAPTER 2

# Harbin: A New World

HSIAO Hung's advanced education began in the fall of 1928,[1] when she was sent to Harbin to attend the First Municipal Girls' Middle School. At that time Harbin was already an important cultural and commercial center in Northeast China; its importance as a city was recognized by a visitor from the West in 1932, who wrote: "Harbin and Dairen [an ocean port city on the southernmost tip of Liaoning Province], as great cities of the modern type, are far ahead of Peking and Nanking, and tend increasingly to rival Shanghai."[2] Owing to its position as a major stop on the Trans-Siberian Railway line, it was also the city in Northeast China most susceptible to Western influences.

It was to this cosmopolitan city, then, that Hsiao Hung came, and she was soon exposed to a whole new set of ideas and a new way of life. The First Municipal Girls' Middle School must have seemed to her father the right place to send his daughter, for it had a fine reputation as a conservative school for girls of good breeding, not at all the sort of place where a girl might be corrupted. And yet, a growing restlessness among youth was manifesting itself in the wake of the major political and cultural changes that were affecting the lives of an increasing number of Chinese; Northeast China, especially the major cities, was virtually a powder keg.

Hsiao Hung's first contact with the youth movement which had sprung up following the 1919 May Fourth Incident came during her first winter term in Harbin in the closing months of 1928. On one cold day she and her classmates were attracted to what grew into a tumultuous noise beyond the school wall; it was a political demonstration by the students of the city. The sheer size of the demonstration caused apprehension among many of the four hundred girls who attended the school,[3] but their excitement and curiosity eventually won the day; against the wishes of their terrified principal, they joined the growing demonstration. The object of the students' displeasure, it turned out, was Japanese encroachments on Manchurian territory.

As a girl just recently removed from the sheltered environment of her family compound, Hsiao Hung was largely unaware of her homeland's situation vis-à-vis the Japanese, although the fervor of the male demonstrators with their shouts of "Down with Japanese imperialism!" had an intoxicating effect on her. On the second day the girls did not wait for the boys to continue their activities but organized their own march. Hsiao Hung herself passed out propaganda leaflets to bystanders, an activity which filled her with a sense of elation. Eventually, inevitably, there was a confrontation with the police. As she braced herself for the clash, Hsiao Hung was overpowered by emotions she was at a loss to understand, let alone explain. Shots were fired, some of the demonstrators were slightly injured, and a new slogan was born: "Down with the police!" The second day of demonstrations was the last, and although no tangible results came out of the episode, to Hsiao Hung, and probably many others, it was an unforgettable experience, one which affected their lives for years to come.

What little can be learned about Hsiao Hung's less spectacular activities and daily regimen at school is supplied by Lo Pin-chi in *A Short Biography of Hsiao Hung*. [4] He writes that she was a quiet and serious girl, rather a loner, a characterization borne out by what we know of her life prior to coming to Harbin and her later years. Her favorite classes were art, taught by a Kirin youth who had come from Shanghai, and history, taught by a college student from Peking, who introduced his students to some of the most successful examples of the "new literature." Hsiao Hung's feelings for these writings were to develop as time went on, but in her first year of school most of her time and all the spare energy she could muster were devoted to painting.

As we have already seen, Hsiao Hung had a special feeling for the beauty of nature. Her attraction to the "great outdoors" can most certainly be partly attributed to escapism, an escape from the ugliness she saw in the actions and attitudes of so many of the people around her in Hulan; whether she also had a natural talent for painting we cannot know, as none of her paintings survived her. However, her genius at describing scenery in words indicates that her "feeling" toward the world of nature was more than a mere reaction against something unpleasant. Whatever the motivation, she immersed herself in art, spending as much time as her schedule and weather permitted roaming the parks and suburbs of Harbin and painting what she saw. Among her favorite spots was the Ma Chia-kou Park in the city; there she and some of her classmates organized their Rural Nature Painting Club.

At some time during what must have been her second year in school, Hsiao Hung, who had been reading the literary supplement of the Harbin *Kuo-chi hsieh-pao (International Gazette)*, began to develop a fondness for the "new literature," a fondness which was soon to eclipse even her love for painting. She was particularly drawn to the Romantic writings that were in vogue at the time, works that waxed eloquent over the ills of society. Translations of Western literature were especially popular during this period and much of Hsiao Hung's interest in a socially oriented literature was the product of her readings of the works of Western writers.

During the winter vacation of 1929–1930 she returned home to Hulan, carrying with her books by Lu Hsün and Mao Tun.[5] Then in the early spring of 1930 this nineteen-year-old girl who "combed her hair into two small braids and had an oval face with clear features and two big black eyes which had a subtle twinkle,"[6] returned to school in Harbin, unaware that her days of innocence and relative serenity were about to end. In the summer of that year she travelled once again to Hulan, where she discovered that her father had made arrangements for her to be married to the son of a powerful warlord general. It was also around this time that her beloved grandfather died; for her there was no longer any reason to remain at home—in fact, there was every reason to flee—and so in the year that she, in her own words, "reached the age of twenty," she left home for good.

## I  *The Passing of Youth*

Popular (and tantalizingly daring) as fleeing from prearranged marriages *(t'ao-hun)* may have been, for Hsiao Hung it marked the beginning of a period of agonies, the effect of which was a progressive deterioration of her emotional and physical health. Materials covering the ensuing two years are sketchy in the extreme, and the account which follows must remain somewhat tentative; but, by all indications, she returned to Harbin immediately after leaving home and consummated a relationship she had begun earlier with a young man who may have been a teacher at the school.[7] According to the

Northeastern writer, Sun Ling, whose friendship with Hsiao Hung began in 1932, she shared a hotel room with the man named Li in the Tao-wai District of Harbin, happy with her newfound courage and freedom.[8] They probably stayed together in Harbin for several months, but how she occupied her time during this period is unclear. Eventually they went to Peking by train. Again, little is known about her life there, or even how long she stayed, though it is generally agreed that she was abandoned in Peking (Lo Pin-chi tells us that on one occasion the man took her to meet his wife and child,[9] the knowledge of whose existence must have come as quite a blow), and she made her way alone back to Harbin. But before that happened she evidently spent some time attending classes in Peking. Hsü Kuang-p'ing (1898–1968), the wife and former student of Lu Hsün, writes that Hsiao Hung had once told her that she attended a high school attached to the Peking Women's Normal College, which, if true, goes a long way toward explaining her activities over many months in Peking.[10] We can be assured, however, that the axe did indeed fall, probably around the time of the Mukden Incident, and that she returned to Harbin, heartbroken and confused, looking forward to a bleak and indefinite existence and the impending birth of Li's child.

It happened that Hsiao Hung's first real "crisis" occurred at about the same time as the Mukden Incident, a national crisis of monumental importance. A relatively unspectacular incident by itself, it was to have worldwide significance. On the evening of September 18, 1931, an explosion outside the city of Mukden (in Liaoning) destroyed a section of track of the South Manchurian Railway line. The ruling warlord of the area, Chang Hsüeh-liang, had pledged his loyalty to the Nationalist regime of Chiang Kai-shek, and the Japanese vested interests in Manchuria were beginning to feel the pinch. Although they had earlier gained control of Dairen and Port Arthur and enjoyed broad privileges in all of Manchuria, still they were heavily outnumbered, and strong anti-Japanese feelings were making their control of the region less and less tenable. For these and other reasons, it is widely believed that the incident at Mukden was contrived by the local Japanese garrison, whose rapid and disproportionately violent response initiated a series of military clashes that, in a remarkably short time, resulted in the complete Japanese occupation of Manchuria. It was formalized with the founding of the state of Manchukuo in March of the

following year, with P'u-yi, the last emperor of the Manchu Dynasty, resurrected, as it were, and installed as Chief Executive of the
new "puppet" regime. The capital was established at Hsin-ching
(Ch'ang-ch'un) in Kirin.

The significance of the Mukden Incident cannot be overstated;
the conflict which grew out of it was to embroil the nation for the
next fourteen years. National salvation became the new rallying cry,
as a growing awareness gripped the entire populace that the nation's
very existence as a sovereign state was at stake. But at the time
Hsiao Hung was probably much less concerned with the national
crisis than with her own plight.

Initially, upon her return to Harbin, she searched out relatives—
to no avail—and friends and schoolmates for assistance. For a while
she slept at the homes of classmates while they were at school
during the day, existed on handouts, and passed the nights in the
age-old tradition of vagrants, sleeping or resting wherever she found
shelter. It was during this difficult time that the chance meeting
with her brother occurred. Beset by the problems of hunger and
cold, and under great emotional stress stemming from her recent
experiences, an unwanted pregnancy, and rebuffs at the hands of
family and friends, she felt herself totally alienated from society: "I
felt that there was a great distance between me and the rest of
mankind."[11]

Finally, unable and unwilling to return home, too proud or too
ashamed to continue to look to friends and schoolmates for assistance, she had little choice but to find a more permanent place to
stay and perhaps sort out the alternatives open to her. She took a
room in a hotel a scant one hundred yards from the banks of the
Sungari River, a run-down hotel peopled by vagabonds and prostitutes and run by a White Russian. According to Sun Ling, she
became a virtual prisoner in this hotel room, spending the winter of
1931–1932 there as a cold and despondent cast-off; not only was she
unable to pay for her room and board, but she was reputedly by
then addicted to opium, conveniently supplied by the designing
hotel proprietor.[12] The future must have looked very bleak indeed.

## II  *Literary and Social Beginnings*

In an obvious act of desperation, Hsiao Hung, who had somehow
survived the winter but was, nevertheless, at the end of her tether,
sent a letter to the editor of the literary supplement of the *Inter-*

*national Gazette,* asking for help; the letter was received in the early summer of 1932.[13] Fei Lao-p'ei, the editor, personally went to see the writer of this plea for assistance, and as he later recalled to his friend, Sun Ling, he was horrified to discover a very pregnant, dishevelled-looking, and opium-addicted girl who was in debt to the hotel proprietor to the tune of four hundred *yüan,* a considerable sum of money at that time. He immediately attempted to obtain her release at a reduced settlement, but the *hotelier* remained adamant. After weeks of negotiations nature ironically came to Hsiao Hung's rescue. Following the spring thaw and heavy rains, the Sungari River threatened to overflow its poorly maintained banks, and the city was bracing itself for the worst. Capitalizing on the imminent flood, which would inundate the hotel were it to come, Fei Lao-p'ei, by use of reason, cajolery, and outright threats, effected her release for half of the money owed. He moved her into his own home where the first order of business was for her (as well as for him and his wife) to give up the opium habit, and it was at this time that she met Hsiao Chün. The beginning of her rise in fortune now permits a digression, one which will lay the groundwork for the next phase in her life.

Hsiao Chün, the young writer who evidently had a hand in Hsiao Hung's salvation from approaching disaster and was to share her fortunes over the coming half decade, almost defies an attempt at biographical investigation, at least for the first twenty-five years of his life. The account which follows, although sketchy, is the best we can do with the materials available.[14]

Born in 1908 in Yi County, Liaoning Province, Hsiao Chün, whose real name is Liu Chün, was one of two children born to a peasant farmer who, with his two brothers, spent much of his middle and later years fighting in volunteer armies. Hsiao Chün received little formal education and after a checkered youth found at least a temporary niche in the army, serving in one capacity or another in various military organizations from 1925 until 1931. At the time of the Mukden Incident he was still in Liaoning, probably in the city of Mukden. He and a close friend soon thereafter moved to the relatively stable atmosphere of Harbin, staying first in a small hotel. Unable to find work, the two friends soon exhausted their money; meals, or at least occasional scraps of food, were providentially supplied by the sympathetic and bold daughter of the hotelkeeper. Then in March, 1932, Hsiao Chün presented himself at the *International Gazette* office of Fei Lao-p'ei in search of a job.

Asked if he could write, he agreed to give it a try, and the next day submitted a piece, which prompted the editor immediately to offer him a job as a regular contributor with a fixed salary for a pre-determined output. Such an offer was unprecedented for this "cut and paste" literary section. The following day the piece appeared in the newspaper under the pseudonym San Lang, an abbreviation of a nickname acquired during his military days. Hsiao Chün's star was on the rise, and the stage was set for him and Hsiao Hung to meet, an event which occurred around the time of Hsiao Hung's escape from her "prison" room in the summer of 1932, and most likely in the home of Fei Lao-p'ei.[15]

Hsiao Chün, an inveterate woman-chaser,[16] was attracted to Hsiao Hung, though he had competition. He evidently won her favors only after he had forced her to choose between him and another prospective suitor, perhaps his fellow Northeastern writer, Shu Ch'ün.[17] A short (5'2" or 5'3")[18], rugged, and pugnacious man with a square face, piercing eyes, and menacingly arched eyebrows, Hsiao Chün, who was given to drinking, quarrelling, and, on occasion, violence, seems eminently capable of having forced Hsiao Hung's decision. She, on the other hand, tended to be rather timorous, unsure of herself, and at the time was physically and emotionally spent.

Before long Hsiao Hung entered a Harbin hospital to give birth to the child of the man who had abandoned her; she evidently never saw the child and left it in the care of the hospital staff.[19] Upon her release from the hospital, probably in July,[20] she returned to the Fei's home, this time in company with Hsiao Chün, who became the new boarder. A scant two months later, in the fall of 1932, Hsiao Chün, in a fit of temper, went on a glass-shattering rampage in the house, and the couple was asked to move.[21] By that time she too had begun submitting prose to the *International Gazette,* using the pseudonym Ch'iao Yin, and both had become well-known writers in Harbin, the talk of many readers of the *International Gazette.* Hsiao Chün's bad temper, however, resulted in more than the loss of a place to stay; it was also the cause of their severed relationship with Fei. It was an inauspicious beginning.

From this time on until they left Harbin there is a marked increase in materials available to the biographer, especially in their own writings. That they were poor, usually cold and hungry, and often desperate is almost a foregone conclusion. Happy as Hsiao

Hung was with her new status and relative security, disappointment
with her surroundings and her still frail health kept her from being
too optimistic about the future.

The months that followed were no less a trial for Hsiao Chün than
they were for Hsiao Hung. First of all, he was used to finding his
pleasures where he could. Then, even when their writings were
being sold, the going rate was ten cents per one hundred words, a
paltry sum by any standard; now, having fallen out with Fei, even
that meager income had been terminated. If he could no longer
write and get paid for it, and since he was now responsible for the
"child-like"[22] Hsiao Hung, what then could he do? The answer, as
he saw it, was clear—teach. Once he had decided on that course of
action, he advertised for students, being careful not to limit himself
to any particular subject. It worked! He soon had a teen-age student
to whom he was to teach swordsmanship, a skill he had acquired
during his military days. His salary was to be twenty *yüan* a month
plus room and board. So Hsiao Hung and Hsiao Chün moved from
their tiny third-floor hotel room—snow was still on the ground—
into a house next door to Hsiao Chün's student on Market Street,
where they were to stay for the rest of the time they were in Harbin.

Even with a steady, permanent job, their situation was still far
from ideal, as the money received from the one student was insufficient for their needs. When other students were found, their lot
improved somewhat, but few of these students stayed very long, for
the teacher's obvious poverty did not usually sit well with them.
The scarcity of food, fuel for the stove, and medicine continued to
plague the couple. Then, to add to Hsiao Hung's miseries, Hsiao
Chün and his student's elder sister, a schoolmate of Hsiao Hung's
whom she had not known, were altogether too friendly, a situation
that gave rise in her to feelings of anger and envy.

Still, good times were to be had, however infrequently, including
swimming, boating, ice skating, dinners at a shabby restaurant, and
occasional get-togethers with friends. And although it would be
inaccurate to say that Hsiao Hung was as busy as she cared to be and
no longer bothered by loneliness—Hsiao Chün was away a good
deal of the time—she did experience the beginnings of activity. She,
too, was a tutor for a brief time[23] and also took regular lessons in
Russian, though she never became proficient in the language.

Over the Lunar New Year holidays in 1933 the couple was en-
tertained along with others by one of their friends, and from these

gatherings the idea to organize a painting and drama club and to publish a literary magazine was born. Earlier, shortly after Hsiao Hung and Hsiao Chün had taken up together, she had participated in an art exhibit, the proceeds from which were to go to victims of the flood caused by the Sungari River overflowing its banks in the fall of 1932. She contributed two paintings, though neither was sold, and both later decorated her own flat.

The clubs organized in 1933, on the other hand, got off to a fairly promising beginning, particularly the drama club. Then in August Hsiao Hung and Hsiao Chün put together a joint anthology of stories and essays and had them printed. They bound copies of the small volume themselves and distributed them to local booksellers. The title of the collection was *Pa-she* (*Trudging*).[24] It was almost immediately proscribed by the Japanese, and the remaining copies were to prove a cause of concern for the authors, who eventually destroyed the bulk of them. Following this episode, a friend was arrested by the Japanese authorities, throwing all of those who were associated with him into a state of near-panic. The political situation in Harbin was worsening daily; spies were everywhere, most freedoms no longer existed, and youths by the hundreds were fleeing, many to join anti-Japanese militia and guerrilla forces. The drama club, which included both Hsiao Hung and Hsiao Chün (as actors), had by then prepared a limited repertoire and was looking forward to putting on its first play. Permission was given by those who controlled the theaters, but there was a catch: the performance had to be given on a day of celebration in honor of the founding of the state of Manchukuo. Needless to say, this was an unacceptable condition, and by declaring it unacceptable, the group's situation grew even more precarious. It was to be the last straw. Most of those involved, realizing that there were but two roads open to them—stay and resist, or flee—chose the latter, and they made plans to leave. The precise date of their departure is not known, but at some time during the month of May[25] Hsiao Hung, Hsiao Chün, and Shu Ch'ün boarded a train for Dairen, and from there took passage on the *Dairen Maru*, a Japanese freighter, to Tsingtao in Shantung Province.[26] They were now "inside the pass" (*kuan-nei*), in China proper; Hsiao Hung would never return to her native Manchuria.

In all, Hsiao Hung spent just under six years in the city of Harbin, a period which witnessed the Japanese takeover of the whole of Manchuria. These were critical years for her. On the plus side, she had gained freedom from her father's dictatorial control and a measure of independence; she had made several important friendships; and, of course, she had begun to write. But what had all of this cost her? In terms of physical health, they were devastating years. Weakened by her pregnancy, a long period of aimless wanderings, stretches of cold and hunger, and a persistent stomach disorder[27] (not to mention the ravages of opium, if she had in fact been addicted to it), she was never again to enjoy good health. The emotional effects of all that had happened to her were probably even more dire. Certainly her experience with her first lover could in itself have been emotionally crippling. Add to that the months she was alone, and the far from ideal year and a half with the domineering, headstrong, temperamental, and usually self-serving Hsiao Chün, and it is almost difficult to believe that a young woman as introverted, sensitive, and unsure of herself as Hsiao Hung could have survived at all. She did survive, but she was badly scarred. Perhaps the most noticeable effects of these years, outside of her damaged physical health, were strongly developed feminist tendencies, pronounced self-pity, and a further drawing inward. But we must not lose sight of the fact that in this period, as in later years, Hsiao Hung was the chief architect of her own unhappiness. Her decision to stay with Hsiao Chün was naturally a far-reaching one, for much of the grief as well as the enjoyment she later experienced was the direct result of his presence or influence. Hsü Kuang-p'ing has written that Hsiao Hung and Hsiao Chün's meeting and union were, later developments notwithstanding, a boon to both of them.[28] There is, as we shall see, considerable room for debate on the subject.

CHAPTER 3

# The Rise to Prominence:
# Tsingtao and Shanghai

THE city of Tsingtao, located on a southward jutting extension of
Shantung Province at the mouth of Kiaochow Bay on the Yellow Sea, is an important port city, which, like Harbin, has
throughout this century had considerable contact with foreigners.
Leased to Germany in 1898, it was taken forcibly by the Japanese in
1914. During the post-war Paris Peace Conference the Japanese
demanded that the previously German-controlled interests be
turned over to them, a demand which led to the May Fourth
Movement and the ultimate return of Tsingtao and other disputed
territory to China.

Hsiao Hung and Hsiao Chün's decision to go to Tsingtao was
evidently prompted by a summons from someone they had known
in Harbin, someone who had a job waiting for Hsiao Chün. Originally, it seems, they had hopes of going from Harbin straight to
Shanghai, but the prospects of steady work and the opportunity to
leave Harbin now that the situation there was becoming intolerable
made their decision an easy one. Waiting for them in Tsingtao (they
most likely arrived in early June, after a brief stay in Dairen) was
another man who had been summoned to Tsingtao, Mei Lin.[1] He
had been living in Yen-t'ai (Chefoo), a seaport city in northeastern
Shantung, for three years but took a leave of absence to come to
Tsingtao and assume the editorship of a small newspaper, the
*Ch'ing-tao ch'en-pao* (*Tsingtao Morning News*). Hsiao Chün
(perhaps with Shu Ch'ün's help) was to edit the literary page of the
paper.[2] He and Hsiao Hung found a hilltop apartment, from which
they could look out their window and see the ocean on two sides.

Mei Lin took an immediate liking to the couple and consequently
spent a good deal of time at their apartment, often staying for meals

33

and accompanying them when they went out on pleasure excursions. Life took on a more relaxed pace than it had in Harbin, and optimism gradually supplanted some of their feelings of desperation. Mei Lin has described how they looked in Tsingtao; Hsiao Chün, at least, must have cut quite a figure:

San Lang [i.e., Hsiao Chün] wore a narrow-brimmed felt hat, turned down in front and sticking up in back, short pants, straw sandals, a light yellow Russian-style shirt, and girded himself with a leather belt—he looked a lot like a ricksha boy; Ch'iao Yin [i.e., Hsiao Hung] used a torn-off piece of sky-blue satin to tie up her hair, wore a cotton *ch'i-p'ao*, Western-style pants, old leather shoes with the heels worn half way down—looking very rustic.[3]

When reading the autobiographical works of Hsiao Hung or biographical sketches about her one is struck by the almost total absence of lighthearted, carefree moments in her life beyond her youth. A generally barren childhood followed by a period in school in which she seemed to be more serious than her schoolmates, and then the later ordeals in Harbin bespeak a dreary, unhappy life. She would grow even more introverted and suffer more in the years following her departure from Tsingtao. And that is what makes this brief (four to six months) stay in Shantung somewhat unique; for once, as Mei Lin's recollections show, she almost seemed to enjoy life:

We wandered here and there . . . then in the afternoon threw ourselves into the blue ocean at the Hui-ch'üan Beach, crazily swimming all over the place. Ch'iao Yin went out to where she was no more than chest-deep in the water, held her nose with one hand, closed her eyes, and sank to the bottom. After forcing herself to stay down for a moment, she stuck her head out of the water and yelled out while coughing:

"Have I swum a long way?"

"You haven't moved an inch," I said. "Look, do like San Lang; just like a ball tossing around on top of the water."

Ch'iao Yin looked at San Lang swimming with all his energy towards the float, shook her head, and sneered:

"His way's no good, no swimming style at all—just brute strength, nothing but flailing and thrashing around. . . . I have my own style."

Then she held her nose and sank once more to the bottom.[4]

This seemingly insignificant account of a typical outing in Tsingtao affords us a rare glimpse of Hsiao Hung in a lighter mood.

Of more importance, she had begun writing on a nearly full-time basis. While Hsiao Chün spent most of his time at the newspaper office, she was home writing short stories and had even begun work on a novel. After reading the story "Chin ch'eng" (Entering the City) (now lost), her first piece published in the *Tsingtao Morning News*, Mei Lin discovered her real promise as a writer of feeling and honesty, and he asked to see what else she had done; she gave him a copy of *Trudging* to read.[5] He agreed that her writing was distinctively feminine, but, unlike her, he considered it an asset to be developed, not a liability to be overcome. His favorable criticisms undoubtedly proved a considerable encouragement to her. Both she and Hsiao Chün wrote on a regular schedule, applying themselves conscientiously to their work, much to the admiration of their friends.

Meanwhile, the newspaper, which had never gained the sort of popularity the editors had hoped for, began to founder. Mei Lin kept it going as long as possible, but to no avail. Hsiao Chün had seen this coming and in early October had sent a letter to Lu Hsün in Shanghai, asking, among other things, if he could send him some manuscripts. It was perhaps a presumptuous request, but, as will become apparent, he could not have made a better choice. On the ninth of October Lu Hsün answered him, saying that he would look at their manuscripts. Hsiao Hung had just finished recopying the novel she had completed exactly a month earlier, so it was sent together with a copy of *Trudging;*[6] Lu Hsün received them on the 28th.[7] The letter from Lu Hsün seemed encouraging, the prospects for the future of the newspaper were not. Shanghai again beckoned them, especially now that they had made contact with the doyen of contemporary Chinese letters, so they began looking for another Japanese freighter, this time in company with Mei Lin, who had quietly laid the newspaper to rest. By the first of November the trio boarded the *Kyōdō Maru* to make the four hundred-mile trip to Shanghai.[8]

During her brief stay in Tsingtao, as we have seen, Hsiao Hung wrote her first novel, *The Field of Life and Death*, a work which captured the interest of readers throughout the nation upon its publication and has since received much critical attention; she completed it at the age of twenty-three. What else she wrote during the time she was in Tsingtao is not known, for none of the dated pieces in any of her collections come from this period, although several date from the time she was in Harbin.[9]

Exhilarating as the experiences of finishing a first novel, receiving the accolades of friends, and a general new lease on life must have been, Hsiao Hung's physical health improved only slightly during her stay in Tsingtao. Though the couple now seemed to know where their next meal was coming from, money was still a problem, and as the weather turned cool in the fall Hsiao Chün wore whatever warm clothes they owned, leaving Hsiao Hung at home to keep warm as best she could. Inevitably, she developed a bad cough, though Hsiao Chün, of course, was never healthier.

Moreover, noticeable cracks began to appear in the couple's relationship, their unity of purpose notwithstanding. Hsiao Hung's hunger for love and attention, a legacy from her childhood, was being ignored by the insensitive, fiercely independent, and dictatorial Hsiao Chün. During their stay in Tsingtao and throughout their remaining years together he was to assume an attitude of supremacy toward her, one which was demeaning and offensive both to her and to most of their friends. A break was not immediately forthcoming, however, since Hsiao Chün's manliness and ego were well served by Hsiao Hung, while she obviously felt that she needed someone to lean on and had no one else to turn to; consequently, their differences remained submerged for the time being.

## I  Shanghai: Lonely Beginnings

Feeling like a couple of marmots, we had arrived in Shanghai. Who did we know here? Who were our friends? Even the heavens seemed a stranger to us here. At first I wanted to take the eighteen and a half *yüan* we had left and use it as travelling money to go back and be a soldier again. Our dreams of living on our writings in Shanghai were soon abandoned, and all I wanted to do was to leave the two novels we had written with him, and let him do whatever he wanted with them. But before we left we at least wanted to see the one man in whom we had faith; who would have thought that it would be so difficult here just to see someone?[10]

The "him," of course, was Lu Hsün, the man with whom they had corresponded, the man to whom they had sent the manuscripts a week or so before leaving Tsingtao, and the one person in whom they had placed their confidence and hopes. Hsiao Hung and Hsiao

Chün had just received a second letter from Lu Hsün, in which he had acknowledged receipt of their letters and manuscripts and had put off their request for a meeting until it was both convenient and necessary (in his next letter he would be more optimistic about a meeting). In the excerpt given above Hsiao Chün tells us just about everything we need to know concerning the couple's first impressions of Shanghai.

Their first day and night in Shanghai were spent in an inexpensive hostel, and the next day they went to look for more permanent quarters.[11] For Mei Lin, who had visited Shanghai several times, it was as easy as finding a friend in the French Concession; that very day he found a small, but available, room. The next day—their third in Shanghai—he returned to the hostel, only to find that Hsiao Hung and Hsiao Chün had already moved to La-tu Road (Rue de la Tour), also in the French Concession. He found them there, ensconced in an upstairs apartment in a newly constructed red brick building in a quiet area on the edge of the Concession, equipped with a view and a few pieces of furniture loaned them by the landlord. Mei Lin's recollections, although not explicit, indicate that with their apartment, at least, they were happy.

Good friends were a rarity then, so they quickly invited Mei Lin to share their apartment. He refused on the sensible grounds that under such an arrangement no one would get any work done, and he remained adamant in the face of their arguments. The two fledgling writers began working in their new apartment, keeping to a rigorous schedule which they had set for themselves. But Shanghai was not Harbin; it was a new environment and was full of aspiring writers—competition was keen. As their food supply dwindled, their attitudes worsened, and Hsiao Hung complained that no matter what she sent to Shanghai periodicals, nothing materialized, not even a return letter!

Meanwhile, they continued to write to Lu Hsün. In their first month in Shanghai they sent him six letters, each of which was promptly answered. Hsiao Chün used the letters to ask questions concerning Lu Hsün's personal life, discuss matters of mutual interest, and ask advice on how he and Hsiao Hung should best approach their work. For his part, Lu Hsün responded to the questions, often taking the opportunity to air complaints regarding the "so-called writers" in Shanghai who were then taking potshots at him (see below). At one point Hsiao Chün asked about finding work;

Lu Hsün could not help him there.[12] In the same letter, afraid that
the money he had asked friends in Manchuria to send him would not
arrive, he asked for a loan of twenty *yüan;* Lu Hsün could (and did)
help him in this request. Lu Hsün's letters were virtually the "staff
of life" for Hsiao Hung and Hsiao Chün, clearly the only thing that
kept their spirits and hopes alive: "When we first came to Shanghai
we knew no one else but him. We sat in our lonely room and read
his letters; he was the only one who cared enough to give encouragement to those two drifting spirits."[13]

Then, on November 27, Lu Hsün sent an invitation to them to
meet him for lunch on the afternoon of the thirtieth,[14] asking Hsiao
Chün to bring the manuscript of his recently completed novel, *Village in August.* Excitement reigned in their apartment. On the
afternoon of the thirtieth they met at the Uchiyama (Nei-shan) Book
Store near Lu Hsün's home. They were joined at a nearby coffee
shop by Lu Hsün's wife and five-year-old son, Hai-ying. Hsiao Chün
has described his first meeting with Lu Hsün as one which produced mixed emotions: thrilled and uncontrollably nervous at the
opportunity to meet him face to face, they were also distraught to
see how sickly he was and angry at those who had been driving him
to the point where he looked like "a man who was addicted to
opium."[15] As they parted, Lu Hsün took Hsiao Chün's manuscript
and gave him the twenty *yüan* he had asked for. It would still be
several months before either Hsiao Hung or Hsiao Chün finally got
something accepted for publication, but this first meeting provided
the incentive to stay in Shanghai, to write, and to resurrect their
dream and make it come true.

## II   *Lu Hsün and the Shanghai Literary Scene*

By the time Hsiao Hung and Hsiao Chün had come to Shanghai in
late 1934, the city, which for decades had been the industrial and
financial center of the nation, had also become the hub of literary
and cultural activities. For writers, the attractions of Shanghai were
many: of major importance was the presence of large foreign settlements in which dissidents could easily find sanctuary, for in an age
when the most important writers were leftists and, as such, often
the targets of persecution by both the Nationalist Government and
later the Japanese, these autonomous settlements played an important role. Then too, Shanghai, as the financial heart of the country,
provided them with the opportunity to get their works into print, for

major publishing houses and book companies had their headquarters there. Finally, the reading public of Shanghai, the most populous city in China, assured the literary circles an enthusiastic and receptive audience for their works. As a consequence, most major literary figures were, by the 1930's, living and working in Shanghai; foremost among them was Lu Hsün, the man who was to play such a vital role in the life and career of Hsiao Hung.

For Lu Hsün, who had already established himself as a first-rate writer of stories, and was becoming China's foremost critic in the literary world and a hero to the nation's youth, the move to Shanghai in 1927 was necessary though personally distasteful. He was most comfortable in Peking where he could devote more time to his study of the history of Chinese fiction; he did not like Shanghai. Yet it was obvious that if he was to be effective in his attacks on Chinese society, its unenlightened and rapacious leaders, and various elements within the literary movement, he would have to be there. In October of 1927 he arrived there from Canton; this date is critical, for it signals more than just a move in locale, it effectively begins his "years on the left," as Harriet Mills has termed the period from 1927 until his death nine years later.[16]

Scarcely had he settled in Shanghai before he found himself under attack, along with Mao Tun, as remnants of a bygone era whose usefulness to the revolution would be ended unless they effected a change in their ideological direction. His adversaries were former members of the Creation Society, led by Kuo Mo-jo (1892–   ), and the newly founded Sun Society, with the Communist writer Chiang Kuang-tz'u (1901–1931) as spokesman and guiding spirit. The charge, simply stated, was that neither Lu Hsün nor Mao Tun was advocating what to their attackers was paramount to China's future development, proletarian literature. In strictest terms, of course, they were right, and right also in their understanding that their own philosophy of literature could gain real acceptance only through the discrediting of Lu Hsün's and Mao Tun's views and the erosion of their leadership. Lu Hsün, customarily, carried on the battle with gusto, as did many of his supporters, and the energies of the entire literary community were largely spent in such polemical activities over a two-year period. Accommodation was eventually found necessary, and in March, 1930, all sides were brought together in a new organization, the China League of Leftist Writers (Chung-kuo tso-yi tso-chia lien-meng), whose goals were the propagation of native revolutionary literature and an accelerated program of translating the works of progressive Western authors. Lu Hsün was the titular head of the organization, while his friend Ch'ü Ch'iu-pai (1899–1935), was its real moving force.

Following the incident at Mukden a year and a half after the founding of the League, the focus of political activities shifted to Shanghai, where incensed students and other segments of the population were openly defying the Nationalist Government's equivocating posture toward Japan's bold encroachments in the north. Inevitably, a minor incident sparked a Japanese retaliation which, on January 28, 1932, erupted into a general attack on the Chinese neighborhood of Chapei, which bordered on the International Settlement. The area was eventually levelled by bombs at a great cost in human life. Lu Hsün himself was caught in the outbreak of hostilities.

Over the next three years he continued to write, though his attitude vis-à-vis government censorship and other restrictions often caused him personal hardships and made necessary occasional retreats into the International Settlement or elsewhere to gain sanctuary. His health, too, was beginning to fail; the victim of pulmonary tuberculosis, which would eventually kill him, he began to lose weight and was susceptible to lingering colds and fevers. Then, to compound his bitterness, he was distressed by factional disputes within the League of Leftist Writers. It was these petty bickerings, including much sniping at Lu Hsün by people like the Communist theoretician Chou Yang (Chou Ch'i-ying, 1908–   ), and their effect on him that were to incur Hsiao Hung and Hsiao Chün's anger following their first meeting with him on November 30, 1934. From that time on they were to share many of Lu Hsün's problems and his bitterness and would soon become members of his "inner circle," and devoted followers.

### III   Hsiao Hung and Lu Hsün

Before examining the fairly unique relationship that developed between Hsiao Hung and Lu Hsün,[17] some conjectures, based on what we have seen regarding Hsiao Hung's psychological and emotional state at this point in her life, are in order here.

In spite of the fact that she has been characterized by many of her eulogists as a determined struggler throughout her life, a thoroughly modern and strongly defiant woman, closer examination produces a rather different picture, speculative though it may be. After a lonely childhood she had entered school in Harbin as a naïve, unworldly, and indrawn girl. Thus, she was vulnerable in many respects, including the classic "girl alone" sense; she was a girl whom a progressive and attractive young man could rather easily manipulate. Consequently, her break with her family may very likely have been less an act of defiance than simply something she was encouraged to do by the young man with whom she subsequently began cohabiting. From what we know of her wretched physical and emotional state after the abrupt termination of this relationship, her vulnerability can only have increased. Then she met Hsiao Chün; her apparent inability to be decisive, coupled with his brusque manner and supreme self-confidence (some would say arrogance), makes it easy to see how she could have been cowed into whatever relationship he desired. If we are right, then the picture that emerges is not of a battler who defied convention as a matter of course, but rather a young woman with strong sensitivities and growing feelings of self-pity, who was tragically unsure of herself and searching for someone on whom she could depend. In Tsingtao Hsiao Chün had not lived up to her expectations nor fulfilled her psychological needs, and the cycle, which was on its third revolution, was again taking a downward turn. At this point she met Lu Hsün.

Lu Hsün's ready willingness to correspond regularly with the young couple, to read their manuscripts, meet them personally, and eventually undertake to get them published is not surprising when one considers that he felt one of the League of Leftist Writers' most important functions was to search out and introduce new writers, those who could be expected to take over from the old guard. As we have seen, his letters to Hsiao Hung and Hsiao Chün were a real event in their lives; far from being short and business-like, they were full of thoughtful advice, information, and light-hearted banter, and also included occasional invitations to meet with him. His second invitation to them was sent on December 17, this time for dinner on the nineteenth.[18] Other guests that evening included two men who were to become Hsiao Hung's and Hsiao Chün's close friends, Nieh Kan-nu and Yeh Tzu.[19] Hu Feng had also been invited but did not attend.[20] Then on the following day the first piece of really encouraging news arrived: a book company had expressed a willingness to publish *The Field of Life and Death*, and Lu Hsün had sent the manuscript to the Literary Censorship Committee of the Central Propaganda Bureau for approval, after which it could go to press.[21] But bureaucratic machines move slowly; the manuscript remained with the censors for six months, eventually being rejected by them as unacceptable. When it was finally published a year later, Lu Hsün, in his Preface, derided the committee for its unenlightened stance and applauded its subsequent demise.

Early in January, 1935, Hsiao Hung and Hsiao Chün moved to another apartment on Rue de la Tour.[22] Toward the end of the month Lu Hsün began sending their manuscripts to several periodicals, while keeping tabs on the status of *The Field of Life and Death*, and commenting at one point that Hsiao Hung should not be concerned if the manuscript was revised by the censors or publishers, since the important thing was getting it into print.[23] Evidently the delay was affecting her, for Lu Hsün remarked in a letter to Hsiao Chün that it would be useless to try to force her to produce.[24] Then came the good news: the magazine *Wen-hsüeh* would publish one of Hsiao Chün's stories in their March issue, and *T'ai-po* had accepted Hsiao Hung's first piece for publication.[25]

Written on January 26, 1935, this short sketch, entitled "Hsiao-liu" (Little Liu), appeared in the final issue of volume one (March 5, 1935) under the pseudonym Ch'iao Yin. Although *Lu Hsün's Diary* usually includes the amounts he received for manuscripts, no clear reference is made to the payment for this first piece by Hsiao Hung. We can be sure, however, that it was not much and that it was sent to him and not directly to the author—all her early manuscripts were submitted by Lu Hsün, and payment filtered back through him. The entry in *Lu Hsün's Diary* for the fifth of March does state that he invited Hsiao Hung, Hsiao Chün, and Yeh Tzu to a restaurant for dinner, perhaps to celebrate this welcome turn of events.[26] On the way, the party was expanded by the addition of two more people, Huang Yüan and Ts'ao Chü-jen.[27]

Things were beginning to happen for both Hsiao Hung and Hsiao Chün: they had begun to acquire a circle of friends, most of whom were writers and nearly all associates of Lu Hsün; their relationship with Lu Hsün himself was growing more intimate; and their writings were beginning to appear in print on an increasing if not yet frequent basis. In the remaining months of 1935 six of Hsiao Chün's essays and stories were published, while at least two more of Hsiao Hung's appeared. It was, at least, a start. But it was not enough to live on, and in this respect Lu Hsün continued to help.[28] Their correspondence with their patron continued, while personal meetings grew more frequent. On the second of May, Lu Hsün, his wife, and child travelled to the French Concession to call on Hsiao Hung and Hsiao Chün and took them to lunch.[29]

Hsiao Hung's first visit to Lu Hsün's home came on the sixth of November of that same year.[30] After making the hour-long trip by streetcar from the French Concession to Lu Hsün's home in Continental Villa (Ta-lu hsin-ts'un) near North Szechuan Road, she and Hsiao Chün joined Lu Hsün and Hsü Kuang-p'ing for dinner, then talked with them late into the night. This was unquestionably a landmark occasion for her; within a few months she and Hsiao Chün would move to be closer to Lu Hsün, and such eagerly anticipated visits would become almost a daily occurrence.

Important as the relationship with Lu Hsün was to Hsiao Hung personally, of considerable importance also was the long-awaited publication of *The Field of Life and Death* in December, 1935. This novel should have appeared in print earlier, but, as already indicated, it fared badly at the hands of the censorship authorities and, ultimately it was Lu Hsün who arranged to have it published. As early as May or June Lu Hsün had used his own money to publish Yeh Tzu's first collection of stories, *Feng-shou (Harvest)*, as the first volume in his Slave Society series (in which Hu Feng also played an active role); this series was published in conjunction with the Jung-kuang Publishing Company. In August of that year Hsiao Chün's *Village in August* became the second in the series; he used a new pseudonym for this work, T'ien Chün. *The Field of Life and Death* was the third volume (and, incidentally, the last). On November 14 Lu Hsün finished reading the proofs, made some final corrections, wrote a Preface which he sent to Hsiao Hung the following day, and turned the manuscript over to Hu Feng.[31] The following month it was published; it was the first time she had used the name Hsiao Hung in print.[32] Almost immediately Hsiao Hung's and Hsiao Chün's novels were proscribed by the Nationalist Government, a development which, like its American counterpart, "banned in Boston," could only serve to enhance their popularity.[33]

It is now time to turn to an examination of Hsiao Hung's first major work, the novel that was not only to make a "household word" of her name, but which has since been considered by many as her major literary legacy. She was, at the time of its publication, most likely approaching one of the peak emotional periods in her life, and her future probably seemed brighter (to her and to others) than at any time before. She had also discovered in Lu Hsün what she had been seeking for so long, a kind and considerate, understanding and encouraging friend, one who would take on many of the aspects of a surrogate father; it was a role which he, too, consciously or not, seemed prepared to accept. In his last letter of 1935 to the couple he wrote:

I don't often use my personal signature in a published work, as it seems sort of childish to me. But since Ch'iao Yin was so set on it, I went ahead and let them print it with my signature; I wrote it too big, though, so you can have them make it a little smaller. This wife of yours, she seems to have grown a bit since she came to Shanghai, and her two pigtails are a little longer; but still she keeps her childish ways . . . what can we do about her?[34]

## IV   The Field of Life and Death

In her lifetime Hsiao Hung wrote three works which we may classify as novels. *The Field of Life and Death*, her first, is unique in many respects, not the least of which is the fact that only it among the three had any observable effect on the society for and about which it was written. This makes it incumbent upon us to examine the novel from two separate, though certainly not unrelated, standpoints: that of its impact on contemporary readers and its effectiveness as a "call to arms," and in terms of transcending literary qualities and effectiveness as a piece of fiction.

We have touched briefly on the publication of the novel in 1935 as the event that established its author as a prominent literary figure. That such fame came to her almost immediately after the book appeared is not surprising, given the mood of the people for whom Japanese encroachments were reaching intolerable proportions. Moreover, even though there were earlier novels set in Manchuria which dealt with the Japanese issue, *Village in August* and *The Field of Life and Death* were the first really to capture the reading public's interest. The popularity of Hsiao Hung's novel was further insured by its being sandwiched between a Preface by Lu Hsün and a Postface by Hu Feng. Many critics of vastly different political persuasions have since argued enthusiastically, if not always convincingly, that *The Field of Life and Death* is not only Hsiao Hung's finest work, but also her only real lasting legacy, in both the political and literary arenas.

Acclaimed by many of its critics as an effective "account of the initial stages of awareness and resistance of the peasants"[35] vis-à-vis the Japanese invaders, the novel seems to have infused into its early readers a positive anti-Japanese spirit. To what extent this was true can only be dimly ascertained from our present vantage point, although the popularity that Hsiao Hung enjoyed for most of the rest of her life and the countless contemporary references to the novel and its impact on society are clear indications of this fact. What is remarkable, however, is that less than one-third of this short (155 pages) novel concerns the Japanese at all, remarkable when one considers that its initial claim to fame was based on its depiction of the Chinese peasants' struggle against the foreign invaders. That it is the story of struggle is indisputable, but a struggle for or against what? Was *The Field of Life and Death* actually intended by its author to be an exposé of Japanese cruelties which fostered rather than discouraged resistance by impoverished peasants who had been driven to the point of no return, as Hsiao Chün's *Village in August* certainly was? To answer this question, let us turn to the novel and examine what it does—and how well—and how it has been viewed by some of its critics.

Set in the countryside near Harbin in the period preceding and just following the 1931 Mukden Incident, *The Field of Life and Death* is about peasant life in a Manchurian village. It is the story of villagers with their precious land and livestock, for whom life has always been a bitter struggle and whose attitudes toward life reflect the harshness of their existence. The tone of the novel is tragic; the comic or light-hearted relief, on which so many of us depend in reality and in fiction, is conspicuously absent. Like the pathetic miners in Zola's *Germinal*, few pleasures creep into the lives of Hsiao Hung's villagers; occasional idle gatherings or illicit sex among the young are invariably followed by unhappiness, tragedy, or guilt. For the reader, if not necessarily for the villagers themselves, beauty is present in the description of rural landscapes that punctuate the book and in the uninhibited reactions to people and events by many of the villagers; but ugliness, in the form of senseless cruelty and ignorance, lends the brief interludes of beauty a kind of grotesque incongruity. In the first hundred pages we are told that times are worse than they have been before, that the merciless forces of nature and rapacious landlords have put the villagers in worse than usual straits. But somehow the reader feels that it has always been just that way, that the comprehension of such people has always been limited to the simple cycle of "birth, old-age, sickness and death."[36] In *The Field of Life and Death* the reader experiences an ever-increasing heaviness of mood as the bitterness of the peasants' lives unfolds before him. He is witness to a "shotgun marriage" with its tragic aftermath, an aborted attempt by several villagers to confront with violence a rumored rise in land taxes, and a seemingly never-ending parade of painful birth, the agonies of old age, debilitating and catastrophic illnesses, and, of course, death in many forms (suicide, accident, plague, murder, and starvation).

Throughout this first and longest portion of the novel a few characters rise to the surface as their stories are told, but it is the village and not any particular person or family that is being portrayed, a community in action, as it were. The static existence of generations of people seems immutable; only the graveyard—a haunting and recurring image—with its voracious and fearless wild dogs and white bones strewn around disturbed graves, changes its face as it imperceptibly grows larger. But change is on the horizon; one morning a new sight confronts the peasants: an unfamiliar flag flutters above a barracks on the top of a neighboring hill. "The villagers were thinking: What is happening now? Has the Chinese nation had a dynastic change?" (p. 100) It is, of course, a Japanese flag, and with the chapter entitled "The Black Tongue," a new scenario is introduced. And yet, true to the concept that the more things change, the more they stay the same, the cycle of birth, old age, sickness, and death continues relentlessly, except that death comes a bit more frequently and from different causes.

The Japanese "devils" soon drive the people to the point where they can do nothing but resist, and resist they do, though we witness only the nascent attempts to organize and an occasional act of individual courage. Then after one long (and important) digression, the novel ends on a note of hopeful optimism, as Erh-li-pan, the final convert to the cause, abandons his sole prized possession, an aging goat, and stumbles off behind a fellow villager to join up with the resistance fighters. Understandably, it was this final portion of the novel that was heralded by the author's contemporary readers and acclaimed by later Communist critics: "The novel realistically reflects the grievous lives of the Northeastern people during those unstable times, as well as the process of their awakening to the struggle of resistance into which they had been forced."[37]

Before going any further, we must first attempt to resolve the questions put forth earlier: that is, is *The Field of Life and Death* essentially a novel about the birth of resistance and political awareness, one whose primary purpose was to incite its readers to action against the Japanese? If so, has its execution effectively matched its design (or, if not so designed, did it achieve that result in spite of its motivation)? Taking the last question first, we must answer it in the affirmative, as Hsiao Hung's novel was praised by many critics as representative of the type of literature that patriotic writers were urged to produce. *The Field of Life and Death* was part of the foundation on which a decade of anti-Japanese literature was subsequently to be built, even though it treats the burning question of the day in a mere thirty-seven pages, and deals with the Japanese encroachments obliquely and almost gratuitously. It seems, after all, that the author's intention was to write about the lives of peasants in her homeland and of the marginal existence that was most often their lot (something that she would do again later with greater success), drawing upon her own observations and experiences to produce a generally moving, if not always organic, narrative of her subject.

What then was the source of this change in theme? In all likelihood we need look no further than the man whose influence on Hsiao Hung's personal life was already considerable, Hsiao Chün. For him, there were more evil forces afoot than those which had customarily tormented the peasants since time immemorial. As an erstwhile resistance fighter himself, he had easily chosen the villains for his novel, and he was able to write of the peasants' gradual commitment to the struggle, based on his own experiences and personal commitment. Hsiao Hung, on the other hand, had had no such experiences, nor had she any firsthand knowledge of the misdeeds of the Japanese invaders. Not surprisingly, this aspect of the story suffers from her lack of understanding of her material. What little concrete references there are to the various resistance organizations in Hsiao Hung's novel could only have come from Hsiao Chün or his friends.

Generally speaking, the switch of theme in mid-novel and the absence of carefully laid motivation precedent to the beginnings of an uprising, plus the highly romantic and rambling manner in which the final third of the book is written, bespeak the author trying to write something for which she is unprepared. To compensate for an absence of any real cause-and-effect development which would lead to an inevitable conflict between the villagers and their Japanese overlords, she has relied on atrocity stories and rumor, hardly the foundation on which sound historical fiction can be based. She introduces a number of specific instances of cruelty, but treats them with so little feeling and imagination that the reader never finds himself completely immersed in the story. At one point we are told, almost matter-of-factly, that a young girl student has been executed by the Japanese, but after a few tentative statements concerning the reasons for this act, the subject is dropped and never mentioned again. Elsewhere, reports of pregnant women having their bellies slit open and young women being carried off, raped, then slaughtered, emerge from conversations among villagers, but no intensity or tension is built, as the malefactors seldom appear in the novel. The question is not that such brutal things did not happen, but rather that Hsiao Hung has not written a convincing account of them.

Then there is the awakening, the picking up of the gauntlet, as it were, by the brutalized peasants. Again, handled skillfully, this could be the stuff of which gripping fiction is made. But in Hsiao Hung's hands it becomes little more than transparent melodrama; the often-quoted speech by Chao San, one of the leading characters, is typical:

"The nation . . . the nation is lost! I . . . I . . . am old too! You are still young, you go and save the nation! My old bones . . . are useless! I'm an old nationless slave, and I'll never see you rip up the Japanese flag with my own eyes; wait until I'm buried . . . then plant the Chinese flag over my grave, for I am a Chinese! . . . I want a Chinese flag; I don't want to be a nationless slave. Alive I am Chinese, and when I'm dead I'll be a Chinese ghost . . . not a nation . . . nationless slave . . . ." (p. 121)

Further indication of the author's conflict between what she felt she could, and what she (or Hsiao Chün) may have thought she should, write about appears in the form of a twenty-page lapse in the final section of the book, in which the young widow Chin-chih leaves the village for Harbin. Although she barely escapes a confrontation with Japanese soldiers on the road (an attempt to keep the anti-Japanese theme in focus, no doubt), the chapter is actually an isolated portrayal of the girl's wretched existence in a strange city, in which she is forced to mend the clothing of customers at the lowest class opium den, sharing the fate of other hapless women who have reached life's lowest rung. When she discovers the extent of the service she is expected to provide for the male customers, it is too late—she is trapped. This chapter must certainly include a substantial amount of autobiography, but its placement in the midst of the final third of the novel effectively destroys what little intensity of feeling the author has created against the Japanese. By the time the threads are picked up again, it is too late—the novel ends fifteen pages later.

What we have, then, is a picture quite different from that given us by too many critics who, with their myopic vision, view the first one hundred pages of the novel as something akin to a prologue to the arrival of the Japanese, a position which hardly squares with a close reading of the book. Yet we must not lose sight of the fact that *The Field of Life and Death* holds an undeniably important position in the social history of the twentieth century, for its influence on the youth of its day was substantial. For a readership of high political consciousness and relatively little sophistication in the "modern novel," the technical and rhetorical flaws in the work paled in importance beside its social message and emotional appeal.

Does all this mean that *The Field of Life and Death* is a failure? This writer believes that its popularity, its contemporary and subsequent fame, and its impact on Chinese society in the 1930's notwithstanding, it is at least a partial failure in literary terms, though it does not lack some redeeming features; in places it is a highly moving and eminently readable work. This is especially true of the earlier chapters, although the author occasionally rises above her material in the later portion and recaptures the reader's interest, even today. Hsiao Hung writes of her peasants with real compassion; their unfathomable poverty is poignantly depicted, now with bold strokes, now with a few telling details. Yet she is not patronizing, as she often shows how ignorance and cruelty among families and between neighbors can be as great a nemesis as outside forces. She has often captured telling traits of her peasant society and the values they hold dear; this is where the novel's real success lies. In his Preface Lu Hsün writes:

Keen observations and extraordinary writing style considerably enhance the book's beauty and freshness. Its spirit is robust. Even those who have no

taste for literature and the arts and those of a pragmatic bent, if they read
these pages and are exposed to the great misfortunes in them, will find it
difficult to come away unmoved. (Preface, p. 1)

There are, in fact, several highly moving, well-executed episodes
in *The Field of Life and Death*. From the beginning of the book the
villagers' strong ties to their livestock are constantly brought into
focus. For most of them, a horse, an ox, a sheep, or a goat is the very
center of their existence, exceeding in importance even their own
children. And so, when Chao San must give up his ox as compensa-
tion for a thoughtless killing, it is the beginning of the end for him,
and abandoning his beloved goat is Erh-li-pan's most eloquent
statement of dedication to the cause. In Chapter Three Chao San's
second wife, Old Woman Wang, is forced by outstanding debts to
the landlord to lead her aging horse to the knacker's. It is a short
episode which captivates the reader by its emotional intensity as
well as by its starkly hideous scenery.

Passively and listlessly the horse follows its mistress, an unknow-
ing victim of poverty. Old Woman Wang, who in her youth had
gone on several similar errands without any misgivings, now finds
herself having to lead to slaughter a horse which has been a compan-
ion to her for years. Alternating between talking to her horse with
resignation (" . . . after all, wouldn't you sooner or later die of starvation anyway?") and frustrated anger by its occasional balkings, the
old woman's distress and compassion are described with great sensitivity. Then she arrives at the knacker's shed; its appearance to the
tormented woman has a paralyzing effect:

On the wooden fence enclosing it were nailed a great many hides. Near
the eaves of the building a crossbar was supported by two tall upright
stakes, over which several horse and ox hooves tied together with hemp in
pairs were draped, neatly suspended there in forked fashion; looped intestines also hung from it in profusion. Having hung there for many days, the
now blackened intestines had taken on the appearance of rigidly straight
lengths of rope. And then there were the trails of blood running from the
site where those leg bones had been dismembered.

Another tall stake rose up on the southern side near the fence, from
which hung coils of steaming intestines drying in the sun. This meant that
that particular animal had just recently been slaughtered, as its intestines
were still warm!

The entire courtyard gave off an overpowering stench, and amidst this world of stench, Old Woman Wang seemed to have turned to lead. She just stood there as if weighted down, devoid of any emotion.

The old horse, the tawny horse, stood there alone next to the wooden fence, scratching itself by rubbing against a hide nailed to the fence. At the moment it was a horse, but before long it too would be just another hide! (pp. 40–41)

Grotesque as the above scene is, seen in the midst of that carnage, vivid testimony is given to the pathos of the old woman and her horse. After meekly accepting the price offered by the knacker, she leaves her horse and begins the sad walk home; she is stopped by the shouts of men behind her:

"Hey! That's no good! The horse is leaving!"

Old Woman Wang turned and looked back—the horse was following behind her. Not knowing what was happening, it was heading for home as always. Several men with their hideous faces came running out of the slaughterhouse, prepared to lead the horse back in with them. Finally it lay down at the side of the road; it planted itself there as if it had taken root in the earth. There was nothing Old Woman Wang could do but walk back into the courtyard, and the horse followed her back in. She scratched the top of the horse's head, and slowly it lay down on the ground, seemingly about to go to sleep. Suddenly Old Woman Wang stood up and walked briskly towards the gate. At the head of the street she heard the sound of a gate closing. (p. 42)

This moving scene is effective in giving the entire novel its grim tone.

Perhaps the single most powerful theme that runs through *The Field of Life and Death* is the juxtaposition of birth (life) and death. One entire chapter, "Days of Punishment," is composed of scenes of birth, and in no other chapter do the author's feelings come across so strongly and with such clarity. Spring and birth are often depicted and related in fiction, but seldom are they portrayed as Hsiao Hung has portrayed them here. It is this chapter that really lays before the reader a stark field of life and death.

The chapter opens with a springtime scene of a bitch giving birth to a litter of pups. "In the warmth of the season, the entire village was occupied with the birth of its young. Big sows were leading their broods of piglets, squealing and running, while the bellies of others were still big, nearly scraping the ground, their many teats virtually overflowing." (p. 69) But this idyllic pastoral scene is soon shattered by the agonizing cries of a pregnant young village woman rolling painfully on a grass mat on the floor, "unable to muster the final burst of effort in this moment of life and death." (p. 70) She dies tragically in childbirth. Elsewhere midwives are running frantically from house to house assisting in each individual drama as best they can. But it is often to no avail; the author seems to be saying: Look how easily the moment of life becomes the moment of death! Certainly the most personal episodes are those surrounding the shortsightedness and hypocrisy of the men who impregnate their wives only to feel revulsion and hatred over their childbearing, and precious little love for the children they have fathered. The personal bitterness of the author which is evident here gives such episodes a special impact.

Several other themes and moving narratives in *The Field of Life and Death* could continue to occupy us, but a fairly clear picture of the novel should by now have emerged. There remains only a final word on two important aspects of the work—its characterizations and its narrative and linguistic style. It is generally agreed that Hsiao Hung's characters all too often fail to come to life, that they are too predictable and in too many cases little more than caricatures. Of the four major characters in the novel—Old Woman Wang, her husband Chao San, the girl Chin-chih, and the doltish peasant Erh-li-pan, who is a symbol of backwardness and narrow vision—only two approach and on occasion rise to the status of real, believable characters. Not surprisingly, they are the two females, Old Woman Wang and Chin-chih. In the often-quoted line from Lu Hsün's Preface to the novel, he writes: "This is, of course, nothing more than a brief sketch whose narration of events and scenic descriptions are superior to its characterizations."[38] Hu Feng, in his Postface, discusses the literary qualities of the novel in greater detail, and it is worth our while to see just what this well-known contemporary critic had to say about *The Field of Life and Death*. While praising the author's talent for describing rural settings (comparing parts of the novel favorably with the pastoral settings in Sholokhov's *Virgin Soil Upturned*) and lauding her handling of the awakening of the peasants' commitment to overt resistance, he has the following criticisms of her style and techniques:

First, there isn't sufficient organizing of the materials; the entire work comes across as a series of random sketches, without leaving an impression that a central theme is being developed, and thereby preventing the reader from experiencing the tension that he should feel. Second, a great lack of imaginative work in bringing unity to the characters depicted is evident. Looking at them individually, her characters give the appearance of life, but their personalities lack definition, and they tend not to be like other people, thus they fail to truly come alive to the reader.[39]

Hu Feng continues by criticizing some of the author's use of language, but attributes that to insufficient rhetorical experience. His criticisms, like those of Lu Hsün's, are both fair and accurate. On the other hand, although *The Field of Life and Death* was Hsiao Hung's first major work, the mastery of simple yet moving narration that would characterize her finest works in the future, is already apparent in it.

CHAPTER 4

# Shanghai and Japan

## Shanghai: 1936

A T the time of the publication of *The Field of Life and Death* Hsiao Hung had known Lu Hsün for almost exactly one year. During that time, as we have seen, her career as a writer began modestly via the publication of several short and unpretentious sketches, followed by the novel which brought her almost instant fame. Lu Hsün's role in her career to date was of signal importance, as he personally introduced her early writings to periodicals whose editors were his close friends, and then single-handedly published her novel at a time when political and economic concerns made it exceedingly difficult for new and progressive writers to get their works into print. It was his encouragement and support that launched her career, and although the Preface which he wrote for *The Field of Life and Death* constitutes only faint praise, he was obviously impressed with the author's potential. He envisioned a bright future for her, stating in early 1936 that she "is the most promising of our women writers, and shows possibilities of becoming as much in advance of Miss Ting Ling as the latter was in succeeding Miss Ping Hsin."[1] In fact, although he was immensely pleased with the reception accorded both *Village in August* and *The Field of Life and Death* and impressed with the talents of his two young protégés, he stated that *"The Field of Life and Death* seemed a more mature work than *Village in August"* and "in terms of a literary future, Hsiao Hung showed more promise."[2] Lu Hsün's wife has written that he took advantage of nearly every opportunity to recommend both novels to friends, associates, and callers,[3] evidence of which is easy to find: the American journalist Agnes Smedley recalled that Lu Hsün personally recommended Hsiao Hung's novel to her "as one of the most powerful modern novels written by a Chinese woman"[4]; and during an interview with a caller he cited it as exemplary of the type of fiction that strengthened the revolution.[5]

But it was on the personal level that the relationship was most remarkable. Although Lu Hsün had long since stopped writing fiction, he remained perhaps the foremost spiritual leader of China's youth; his attacks on Chinese government leadership, literature, and national traits, though occasionally dripping with needless venom, provided the ammunition for a veritable army of young followers. And yet, as Tsi-an Hsia has concluded, by 1936 Lu Hsün was a bitter, almost paranoic man who desperately needed a coterie of sympathetic listeners around him.[6] In their separate relationships with their patron, the two Northeastern writers were a study in contrasts: Hsiao Chün, the volatile and fervent revolutionist and patriotic intellectual, was ideologically committed to the struggle in which Lu Hsün was embroiled: Hsiao Hung, on the other hand, was most comfortable in the traditional feminine mold, finding in Lu Hsün someone who supplied her with the emotional security she so desperately needed. There is certainly no indication that her ideological interests ran as deeply or were as well defined as Hsiao Chün's and most of the young men around Lu Hsün; and even her feminist views took on less importance to her under the emotional solace she found in Lu Hsün's house.

One of the couple's first acts in 1936 was to move from the French Concession to an apartment on North Szechuan Road within walking distance of Lu Hsün's home. From that time on for several months, "every evening after dinner we almost never failed to make a trip to Continental Villa, even on windy or rainy days."[7] The several months during which Hsiao Hung was—after Lu Hsün's younger brother, Chou Chien-jen,[8] and his family—perhaps Lu Hsün's most frequent visitor, must have been, all things considered, the most nearly idyllic period in her adult life. In effect, she became a member of the family, rather than just a guest, one who played with the boy Hai-ying, cooked, and kept both Lu Hsün and his wife company. Hai-ying was especially fond of Hsiao Hung, Lu Hsün once remarked, because her pigtails and almost child-like demeanor made her, in the young boy's eyes, a playmate.[9]

We must not be led to the conclusion, however, that her troubles were by this time entirely in the past, for such is not the case. In terms of general physical health, she was not proving as resilient as she had probably hoped to be. Hsü Kuang-p'ing has given us a detailed look at the state of Hsiao Hung's health during her stay in Shanghai: at their first meeting she noted with amazement the young woman's pallid face and graying hair. Later Hsiao Hung often complained of frequent headaches, a general weakness, and gave the appearance of being seriously anemic. What's more, she continued to be bothered by a lingering stomach ailment and, what was to prove more serious, a menstrual problem, for which Lu Hsün's wife recommended a proven medication.[10] Her cough, which had plagued her in Tsingtao, evidently disappeared, as no mention of it is made by any of the writers who knew her in Shanghai. But if most of them generally overlooked the subject of her physical health, few have been so remiss in terms of her emotional situation. Hsiao Hung had come to Shanghai with a host of bitter memories; her subsequent satisfying relationship with Lu Hsün and his family most likely took the edge off most of them, but not all. Once again, we turn to Hsü Kuang-p'ing, who as a close friend and, more importantly, a woman, was privy to a side of Hsiao Hung that others could only guess at. For all their enjoyable times together, there were also many occasions when Hsiao Hung was in a depressed state, complaining of loneliness, ennui, and frustration, occasions when either Lu Hsün or his wife spent hours keeping her company, trying to dispel her anxieties. The source of her emotional ills during this period can only have been her worsening relationship with Hsiao Chün, whose overpowering protectiveness, intellectual disdain, and physically demanding attitude toward her contributed to a loss of self-confidence on her part and was physically damaging to her as well.

But whatever her personal situation, Hsiao Hung did not neglect her writing career, and after the success of her first novel her manuscripts were welcomed by magazines and publishers alike. Less than a year after the appearance of *The Field of Life and Death*, a second book by Hsiao Hung, *Market Street*, saw publication.

## I  *Market Street*

In the eyes of many literary critics who have written about Hsiao Hung, the excellence and importance of *The Field of Life and Death* have overshadowed everything she wrote subsequent to it; although many of her later works are treated favorably, they still fail in her critics' eyes to match her initial effort. In recent years this trend has lost some of its momentum, and many writers have begun to examine more closely her later writings, thereby producing some interesting observations and conclusions. Her nonfiction work *Market Street*, however, continues to be disregarded by critics and has been the most singularly neglected of all her longer works. It is a curious and, in this writer's opinion, unwarranted omission, for there is some indication that it was a popular book during the author's lifetime,[11] having undergone a second printing a month after its initial publication by the Wen-hua sheng-huo Publishing Company in August, 1936. More importantly, its very excellence should dispel the notion that only Hsiao Hung's novels should rightfully earn her a place in contemporary Chinese letters, for *Market Street* exhibits many of the same qualities that her finer works of fiction possess and certainly makes for as enjoyable reading as any of the latter.

*Market Street*, which was completed in May, 1935, and published under the pseudonym Ch'iao Yin, is autobiographical, the title being the name of the street on which the author and Hsiao Chün lived during their last year and a half in Harbin; it is a chronological account of their lives during this period. But it goes far beyond the bounds of traditional autobiography, in that Hsiao Hung has applied her uniquely feminine and personal touch to capture the atmosphere, the moods, and the often-overlooked details that bring such accounts to life. Her effortless recall of events, both major and minor, that were part and parcel of her life in those months, and the beautifully simple writing style which was her hallmark throughout her writing career combine to make *Market Street* a highly successful work. Trying as that period in the author's life had been, there is a notable lack of self-pity in her account; contrariwise, the dominant mood, their poverty notwithstanding, is one of stoic resignation fortified by dogged optimism. She has succeeded in capturing the anxieties and suspense that she experienced, as well as the infrequent humor and lighthearted diversions that helped balance the couple's unenviable situation. Much as she was later to make Lu Hsün and the peasants in Hulan come to life for her readers, she has succeeded in *Market Street* in doing the same for both Hsiao Chün and herself, and in a way that she was never quite able to do in her fictional characters. This is, of course, an extremely important phenomenon, as it would be one of the keys to the success or failure of her later works and, had she lived longer, a clue to the direction her literary career would have taken.

Many parts of *Market Street* are strikingly reminiscent of George Orwell's true account of his own experiences as a penniless young man in Europe, *Down and Out in Paris and London*, a book which was written at about the same time as *Market Street*. One witnesses here the same demeaned existence of the dispossessed poor, the unique camaraderie of people who must constantly scrounge and compromise for food and lodging, and the overpowering psychological effects constant hunger has on them. Both accounts describe not only the personal vicissitudes of their authors, but paint a sobering picture of poverty in general. There is little else which can (or should) be said in general terms regarding *Market Street*; it is time to let the author speak for herself.[12]

One of the chapters in the book is laconically entitled "Hunger"; it is a recurring theme, and one of the most vividly described. Like so many poverty-stricken people, Hsiao Hung and Hsiao Chün were often reduced to existing on black bread and salt alone, when they could afford even that. Though it is difficult for anyone with a full belly to relate to scenes of hunger, Hsiao Hung's very personal descriptions of what food means to a desperately hungry person are most effective:

The following day that big basket stuffed with bread was waiting for me on the street outside. I didn't even open the door a crack, but there were others out there beyond my door buying some, and even with the door closed, I thought I could smell the aroma of wheat. I began to have a fear of bread; it's not that I had a desire to eat any bread as much as I feared that I was being swallowed up by bread! (pp. 28–29)

Like Orwell, she comes to the realization that besides the obvious physiological and psychological effects of constant hunger, intense boredom gradually overcomes its victims; their obsession with their bellies makes them incapable of performing almost any normal activity. In one particularly revealing episode, Hsiao Hung recounts her conflict between hunger and virtue, as she spends an agonizing morning contemplating the theft of a neighbor's food. Elsewhere she describes the importance of melon seeds to a person who has missed several meals; the occasional orgy of eating when she and

Hsiao Chün have money; and, as a humane and sensitive person, the distress of others in similar predicaments. In fact, the wretchedness of beggars fills the author with feelings of deep-seated pity, frustration at her own inability to help, and outraged anger at the callousness of others:

> A woman was standing in the doorway of a pharmacy begging money, holding one child by the hand, with another smaller child bundled up in the wide sleeve of her coat. No one in the pharmacy paid her any attention, nor did any of the passersby, as if they were thinking that it wasn't right for her to have any children. Poor people shouldn't have children, and if they did, they deserved to starve!
>
> I could only see one side of the street outside; the woman had probably walked over to stand beneath my window, because I could tell from the children's crying that they were close by.
>
> "Sir, madame, have pity . . . please have pity. . . ." I couldn't see whom she was addressing, but even though I was on the third floor, I could hear her quite clearly, and I was sure that she was running here and there as she pleaded: "Sir . . . sir . . . won't you take pity on me?"
>
> I'm sure we were in the same predicament, neither one of us having had breakfast; maybe she hadn't even eaten the night before. Her urgent pleading was contagious, and my own stomach started to growl, my intestines made churning noises.
>
> Lang Hua [Hsiao Chün] still hadn't returned; what was there for me to eat? How about the table? Or what about the straw bedding? (pp. 33–34)

As in *The Field of Life and Death*, the delights of spring lose some of their luster under Hsiao Hung's scrutiny:

> Listen, just listen, the song of spring is in the air . . .
>
> "Sir, madame . . . help me please. . . ." What kind of song is this? Is it coming from behind? This isn't a song of spring!
>
> The beggar was eating a rotten pear, and one of his legs and the foot were so swollen that the other one didn't seem to exist at all.
>
> "My leg, it's frozen! Please, sir, help me! Ai! Ai! . . ."
>
> Who could still remember winter, with the sun's rays now so warm, and buds on all the trees? (p. 116)

Elsewhere the author turns her attention to her own plight as a virtual prisoner in her room; she often gives voice to complaints of loneliness, frustration, and ennui, with which women throughout the world doubtless sympathize; and there are other familiar scenarios:

When he brought the firewood home, I began lighting a fire, and there, standing beside the stove, much to my surprise, I began cooking dinner, just like a little housewife. I scorched the vegetables, and the rice was half-cooked. If we called it gruel, then it was too chewy; if we called it steamed rice, then it was too sticky. And so I became a "housewife"; otherwise, how could the fact that I was cooking a meal be explained? . . . (p. 42)

There are light episodes, such as their successful attempts to make a match between a beautiful neighbor girl and an erstwhile misogynist, but mainly the mood is more serious. *Market Street* shows Hsiao Hung to be a distinctively feminine writer who is occasionally sentimental (though seldom do we witness the dripping sentimentalism that characterizes the writings of authors like Ping Hsin) and unabashedly candid. These traits, plus her genius at perceptive observation and an unadorned writing style are qualities that appear in most of her writings, though *Market Street* is perhaps her most personal work and in many respects one of her most powerfully moving.

## II  *Renewed Literary Battles*

Mid–1936 found the literary circles of Shanghai in a turmoil, as a new round of debates was being waged among the leftists. Since these debates consumed so much of the energies of Lu Hsün and others, a brief digression to examine this episode and its consequences is in order here.

In June of the previous year Ch'ü Ch'iu-pai, the behind-the-scenes leader of the League of Leftist Writers, had been executed by the Kuomintang Government. By the end of the year anti-Japanese feelings throughout the nation were reaching a fever pitch (*The Field of Life and Death* and *Village in August* certainly contributed to the mood), and calls for a united resistance to the aggressors were growing in intensity. The Communist Party had taken just such a stand, publicly advocating a united National Defense Government. This turnabout signalled the end of the now leaderless League; national unity was inconsistent with its call for unity among leftists only, and writers of all persuasions were being urged to concentrate their efforts towards national salvation. And so, in the spring of 1936 the League simply ceased to exist, a fact that its titular head, Lu Hsün, learned about only after it was a *fait accompli*. Injurious as this must have been to his ego, his relations with the League during the latter half of its existence had been far from cordial. Dedicated to its founding principles, he was, nonetheless, distressed by the factionalism that continued to exist within the organization as well as by many of its policy pronouncements. He had advised against Hsiao Chün's membership in the League[13] (neither Hsiao Chün nor Hsiao Hung ever became a member) and often complained to his correspondents about its activities and intrigues. What followed the League's demise, however, was far from harmonious. A bitter (and, some observers would say, pointless) battle of polemics erupted, sapping the energies of a large segment of the creative literary society and leaving scars, many of which never healed.

On June 7, 1936, the slogan "National Defense Literature" was officially adopted by a newly created Chinese Writers' Association, an organization that had a membership of over a hundred; conspicuously absent from the manifesto were the names of Lu Hsün and most of his loyalists. He felt betrayed, as his staunchly proleftist stance was threatened with being discredited, and so the battle was joined. Less than a month later, on the first of July, a counter-manifesto was issued in the name of the Chinese Literary Workers, advancing a slogan devised by Lu Hsün in collaboration with Mao Tun and others. The new slogan, unwieldy but sufficiently limiting to Lu Hsün's tastes, was "People's Literature for the National Revolutionary Struggle." Hsiao Hung, Hsiao Chün, and most of Lu Hsün's circle were signatories. Eventually Mao Tun, who had signed both manifestos, intervened as mediator between the two sides with the result that the invective ceased and a compromise was struck. In early October a new manifesto was issued under the heading "Literary Workers' Manifesto on the United Resistance and on Freedom of Speech," with twenty-one signatories, Lu Hsün and many of his erstwhile enemies among them. Neither Hsiao Hung nor Hsiao Chün participated actively in the debates, though both *The Field of Life and Death* and *Village in August* were held up as representative works in support of *both* contending sides![14]

Even during such stormy times the creative drive in many of the participants proved irrepressible (if, perhaps, blunted), and literary writings continued to appear. Nineteen thirty-six was a particularly fertile year for new literary periodicals, with as many as four major magazines appearing in Shanghai alone. The four were: *Tso-chia*, *Wen-chi yüeh-k'an*, *Kuang-ming*, and *Chung-liu*. The appearance of these magazines proved especially advantageous to Hsiao Hung and Hsiao Chün, as three of them (*Kuang-ming* excluded) were the vehicles for nearly everything they published through mid–1937.

### III   The Bridge

One month after the final resolution of the debates over National Defense Literature, and three months after the appearance of *Market Street*, the Wen-hua sheng-huo Publishing Company brought out *The Bridge*, a collection of thirteen short stories and sketches written by Hsiao Hung between late 1933 and early 1936. Three had been published previously. Like *Market Street*, *The Bridge* appeared under the pseudonym Ch'iao Yin, and it also seems to have been well received, as it underwent three printings by early 1940. The range of subject matter and quality in this collection is substantial, making an overall assessment nearly impossible; nevertheless, we shall look critically at several individual pieces. There are but two works of short fiction in *The Bridge*, including the title piece and "Shou" (Hands). Both are quietly sad stories, and both show promise, though the latter is far and away the better work.

"Hands" is an extremely moving story of a country girl's short-lived residence in a school, and is at once a commentary on the devastating evils of elitist cruelty and a touching study of their effect on an all-forgiving and self-effacing peasant girl. Wang Ya-ming is, from her very first day at school, treated as a pariah by classmates and teachers alike, partly owing to her conspicuously blackened hands and partly because of her humble origins, rustic ignorance, and naïveté. The second eldest daughter in a family of dyers, she has been given the cherished opportunity to get an education. But the education she receives in the time she spends in school before being told to leave is not what she expected. By far the most industrious girl in her class, she nonetheless finds too many obstacles thrown in her path, more than she can overcome. Most of Wang Ya-ming's problems come not from her own shortcomings, but from the derisive attitudes of her schoolmistress and her fellow-students. Spending every waking minute with her studies and lamenting her own denseness with disarming honesty, she nevertheless suffers the ignominy of having to sleep on a hallway bench as an outcast and the constant belittling laughter of her classmates. But it is the headmistress who has the talent of reducing her to tears:

"Can't you wash those hands of yours clean? Try using more soap! Give them a thorough scrubbing and soak them in hot water. At morning drill on the playground, when hundreds of white hands go up, you're the only one who's different. A real freak!" With transparent fingers, like some bloodless fossil, the headmistress tapped Ya-ming's black hands, holding her breath rather fearfully, as if forced to pick up a dead crow. "The color's worn off a good deal—you can see the skin on the palm now. That's much better than when you came; your hands looked like iron then. . . . Are you keeping up with your studies? You must work harder. From now on you needn't attend morning exercises. Our school wall is low, and in the spring there are a good many foreigners who stroll past, and often they stop to look over the wall. You may join in the drill again when your hands are white." (pp. 111–12)

And with that, the coming of spring finds Wang Ya-ming restricted to her room, though she accepts even this with a resignation born of determination and poverty. Then, finally, just before her widowed father comes to take her home for the last time, Wang Ya-ming talks about her hands, and in the process says a great deal about her life:

"From that time on I had to look after my two younger brothers and two younger sisters. Father dyed the black and the blue things, while my elder sister dyed the red ones. Last winter, when my elder sister's marriage was arranged, her future mother-in-law came in from the country to stay with us. At first sight of my sister she cried: 'Ai ya! She has the hands of a murderer!' After that, Father wouldn't let any one of us dye only the red things, or only the blue things. My hands are black, but if you look carefully you can see traces of purple. My two younger sisters are the same." (pp. 128–29)

In "Hands," to the credit of the author, she has, somewhat untypically, limited the scope of her subject and has succeeded in creating a fine short story. Wang Ya-ming is a more successful character than anyone in *The Field of Life and Death*, one whose story is of compelling interest.

"The Bridge," the other story in the collection, is more ambitious, carries a stronger message, and is considerably less effective. The story of a nanny to the son of a well-to-do family, it traces the woman's relationships with her young charge and with her own son.

Running between the woman's own house and that of her employers is a water-filled ditch, across which a bridge has been constructed to connect the two banks. For years, however, the bridge flooring has been missing—there remain only the two railings—and a long walk to the end of the ditch is required each time she goes from one house to the other. This ditch symbolizes the gap between the two families, and the bridge over which no one can cross is another obvious symbol ("If only the railings, too, had disappeared, then she would have felt easier about it; then she could believe that the ditch was a natural one, and that man would be powerless to conquer it." (p. 17)). This story, in fact, seems to be Hsiao Hung's first conscious attempt at symbolism, something she uses with a heavy-handedness that detracts from its efficacy. The woman's name is Huang Liang-tzu, an extension of her husband's name, Huang Liang; their son is called Little Liang-tzu. *Liang* means "virtuous" or "good," whereas the foxtails (tares) growing on the master's wall carry the connotation of evil ("The foxtails atop the master's wall were getting plump, while on the eastern side of the bridge, the crying sounds of Huang Liang-tzu's child grew louder." (p. 19)). In addition to its overly-conspicuous symbolism, there are other serious flaws. There is, first of all, a real problem with the author's handling of time; poor transitions and a lack of clarity in respect to time often introduce an element of confusion, as do several generally unclear passages throughout the story. Mostly, however, it is the forced sentimentalism which makes it only a second-rate effort. There is, for example, the melodramatic final scene where the woman's son has fallen into the ditch and drowned, caused in part by the recent construction of a new and usable bridge near the site of the old one:

That day Huang Liang-tzu heard her child fall into the ditch, and frantically she ran down to the water's edge. When she saw that her child was no longer breathing, after having been dragged up to the bank of the ditch, she stood up and looked over the heads of the bystanders in the direction of the bridge.

Those quivering bridge railings, those red bridge railings; in her confusion she thought she saw two sets of bridge railings.

Then the lungs in her chest heaved and expanded. This time she was truly crying. (p. 36)

Huang Liang-tzu is the only real character in the story—there is no dialogue. She occasionally speaks to the children or to her husband, but they themselves are silent (with one or two brief exceptions). The story alternates between narrative and the interior monologue of the protagonist; the following passage is typical:

She took hunks of steamed dough, biscuits, and sometimes even stuffed dumplings and nameless snacks that gave off a greasy odor, and tossed them from the western side of the bridge over to the eastern side.

—Separated only by a bridge . . . otherwise . . . couldn't he be eating these things any time at all? You poor little devil, in your destiny there should have been a bridge!

Every time whatever it was she was tossing over fell into the water she said to her child on the eastern side:

"You poor little devil, in your destiny there should have been a bridge."

The master never once saw her tossing things over to the eastern side of the bridge. But whenever a ripple spread across the surface of the water it frightened her so much that it seemed as though she were seeing the reflection of her own heart in a mirror.

—It's clear as can be . . . these things are stolen. . . . (p. 23)

In summary, "The Bridge" is a tragic story, centered on the inequality between the rich and the poor, but one which, through comparatively inept handling by the author, seems somewhat unconvincing.

The prose sketches which compose nearly two-thirds of the volume are a mixed bag, although they are all, to some extent, personal reminiscences. They range in time from a childhood reminiscence in Hulan, to Harbin—both before and after the author met Hsiao Chün—and Tsingtao. In terms of interest and readability, too, the range is wide. Some, such as the piece "Kuo yeh" (Passing the Night), which concerns the author's cold and hungry existence in Harbin, and "Fang-wen" (The Interview), which deals with a Russian émigré in Harbin, are extremely disjointed. Others, like "San-ko wu-liao jen" (Three Bored Men) and "Li-ch'ü" (Going Away), say practically nothing. In many of the pieces quite strong anti-male sentiments are apparent; they will enter our discussion later. One of the most enjoyable sketches is "Crouching on a Ricksha," which recounts an episode in which Hsiao Hung's grandfather struck a ricksha-puller, thereby damaging his image in his granddaughter's eyes. Two of the sketches set in Harbin are perhaps the most enjoyable and among the most skillful; not surprisingly, they are pure autobiography. The account of the author's chance meeting with her younger brother in Harbin, "Early Winter," has already figured in our discussion. In "P'o-lo chih chieh" (The Ghetto Street), the reader is back on Market Street; the scenario is the same—hunger and boredom—and the style is the same, but there is a new twist, a note of social consciousness:

> It's been a year since we came to this ghetto street. Now our standard of living is higher than it is for these people; we have pulled ourselves up out of the mire. But they stay there forever; they spend their whole lives being submerged there, and their sons and grandsons as well. Just how long will they be submerged there? I wonder.
> And us, we're no better than dogs, that's how much feeling we have. We've pulled ourselves up out of the mire, but we have forgotten others, we've forgotten them! (pp. 55–56)

## IV   Japan: Disillusionment and Sorrow

Nineteen thirty-six, the year which began so auspiciously for Hsiao Hung, turned dark for her at the height of her success. There were two reasons: her worsening relationship with Hsiao Chün and the death in October of Lu Hsün. During the first half of the year she had expanded her circle of friends and acquaintances to include such people as Mao Tun, Agnes Smedley, and dozens of other young writers, editors, and publishers, all of whom she had met through Lu Hsün. She had by then become a successful writer herself. At home, however, an already difficult relationship with Hsiao Chün was being strained to its limits, and by mid-year Hsiao Hung had decided to take the drastic step of leaving him. Of equal concern to her was the precarious condition of Lu Hsün, who was weakened by several illnesses, most prominently tuberculosis. In May, as the battle over National Defense Literature loomed menacingly on the horizon, his health took a serious turn for the worse, and there was widespread concern over his failing condition.

June was to be his worst month; during that period (June 6–29) he ceased making entries in his diary and believed himself to be on the verge of death. In July the crisis passed and he regained some of his vigor; he was soon back at work on about the same schedule as before. Then on July 15 he made the following terse entry in his diary: "Evening, Kuang-p'ing prepared a farewell dinner for Ch'iao Yin."[15] Hsiao Hung had come alone, and soon after she left for Japan alone.[16] Ten days later Hsiao Chün, too, went to see Lu Hsün,[17] his last recorded visit for three months; by September he was back in Tsingtao.

At this point two obvious questions confront us: first, irrespective of her emotional or physical state, from what we know of Hsiao Hung's feelings toward Lu Hsün, how could she have left him at a time when his health was so precarious, and, second, what could have motivated her to choose Japan, of all places, to flee to? The answer to the first question can only be that, in her eyes, Lu Hsün's "crisis" had indeed passed, and there seems to have been justification for her belief. Feng Hsüeh-feng, one of Lu Hsün's closest friends, has written that his seeming recovery in July was most encouraging, and while no one believed that his health problems were over, his friends all felt that the worst had passed. His death three months later was met with almost total disbelief by even those closest to him.[18] This would certainly explain Hsiao Hung's willingness to leave Shanghai at that time.

Any answer to the second question, on the other hand, is much more speculative. It is clear, first of all, that her decision to leave Shanghai stemmed not from poor physical health, but from an irresolvable emotional crisis, though health would make a good pretext. But why Japan? If irrationality is not the answer, we must look again to Lu Hsün. His antipathy toward the Japanese militarist government aside, many of his closest personal friends in Shanghai were Japanese, including Uchiyama Kanzo; his personal physician, Dr. Sudō; and Kaji Wataru.[19] It thus seems plausible that Japan was chosen on Lu Hsün's recommendation and that arrangements for the trip and for Hsiao Hung's stay in Japan were made by him or by his Japanese friends. For Hsiao Chün such a choice would probably have been unthinkable; for Hsiao Hung, however, with whom political considerations did not weigh so heavily, it would not have seemed so distasteful.

Little is known of how Hsiao Hung occupied her time once she arrived in Japan, though a few details have come to light. She lived in Tokyo alone and attended classes of some sort.[20] She never became proficient in the Japanese language and most likely associated with members of the Chinese community in Tokyo, some of whom were overseas students from Manchukuo. She admits to having had but one friend in Tokyo, perhaps a classmate, whose name, Yi-lin, indicates that she was not a Japanese.[21] But the details of her life there, such as we can determine, are less important than what she accomplished there and what effects her brief stay had on her.

Whatever benefits she may have derived from her months in Japan, they were more than offset by the constant overpowering loneliness and unhappiness she felt, away from her friends and her native country in what was, at best, a passively hostile environment. No clearer testimony to her isolation is needed than that available in the short piece she wrote in Tokyo on August 9, 1936, "A Lonely Life":

At dinnertime . . . I went out and bought some things and brought them home to eat; as usual, some bread and ham.

After I finished eating, I was overcome by a feeling of loneliness. Thunder rumbled outside, and the sky was dark and foreboding. I felt like going out for a walk, but was afraid it would rain; if I didn't, though, the night would be even longer than the day, with me cooped up here in my room. So finally I put on my raincoat and went out. I would have done some window shopping at the night market, but as I was still afraid that it might rain, I decided to go visit my friend Hua [Yi-lin?]. I walked over there with all my presentiments of disappointment. As expected, she hadn't returned home yet; once again I spotted her slippers lined up there, and once again I could hear the unintelligible mutterings of her landlady.

If, just if, I had any other friends or acquaintances, I would have gone to look them up, even if it had started to rain. But there wasn't a single one, so there was nothing else to do but go back home the way I had come.[22]

One would think that life in Shanghai, with all its problems, must have looked pretty good to her by this time. As a matter of fact, in the same sketch she admits that for her the quietude of Japan was, if anything, disquieting:

After cleaning up my room,. I decided to do a little work. And here is where Japan and our homeland, China, differ; even though there were already sounds of *geta* on the street, the houses were all so quiet they seemed to be sleeping. I picked up my pen, planning to write something or other, but before I began I had to think about what I wanted to write, and as soon as I began thinking, I forgot everything instead.

Why is it so infernally quiet! All this quiet is disturbing to me.

So I went outside and walked around; the street, too, was different than those back home in China—too quiet, just like everything was asleep. (p. 93)

Not all of Hsiao Hung's attempts to "write something or other" were foiled by her environment or her mood, although some, if the truth be spoken, perhaps should have been. In the months of September and October, 1936, five stories and sketches were published in Shanghai magazines, all but one of which are noted as having been written in Tokyo. They were subsequently published in book form by the Wen-hua sheng-huo Publishing Company, and although the collection, entitled *On the Oxcart*, did not appear until mid–1937, we shall look at it now in the context of her stay in Japan.

### V   On the Oxcart

In *On the Oxcart* the reader is again confronted with a wide range of style, length, and quality. The first piece to be published, on the fifth of September, in the inaugural issue of *Chung-liu*, was a sketch about the author's loneliness in Tokyo, "A Lonely Life," from which we have already seen excerpts. Ten days later the shortest piece in the collection, "Hung ti kuo-yüan" (The Red Orchard), was published in the magazine *Tso-chia*. It is a slow-moving, lightweight piece about unrequited love and gives evidence of the author's pessimistic bent at the time of its writing. The subject is a schoolteacher whose love parallels the coming to maturity of the trees in the orchard outside the narrator's window, but, unlike the trees, ultimately bears no fruit. Before the reader has had time to stifle a yawn, the piece blessedly ends. It is followed (chronologically) by a frantic little story, "Wang Szu ti ku-shih" (The Story of Wang Szu), which, in the space of eight pages, traces the thoughts, eccentricities, and anxieties of an aging menial who lives more in the past than in the present. Unhappily, the reader never has a chance to become involved with the ephemeral and, at the end of the story, heroic Wang Szu.

The title story of the volume, "On the Oxcart," was first published in the October issue of *Wen-chi yüeh-k'an* and is generally considered to be one of Hsiao Hung's most successful stories. To put it in perspective, it is a better story than "The Bridge" but inferior to "Hands." The heroine, Wu-yün Sao, is also a woman who has been the victim of a personal tragedy, this time the death of her husband who was executed as a military deserter. She tells her story to the narrator, a girl whose family employs her as a maid (perhaps Hsiao Hung's own family), and the driver of the ox-drawn cart on which they are all riding. The author has succeeded in involving the reader in the emotional torment of the woman as well as in the suspense surrounding the anticipated delivery of her husband to the local barracks where the entire band of deserters is to be executed. Her use of flashback and the contrast of the drama which unfolded years before with the peaceful and uneventful ride in the country add to the success of "On the Oxcart." Surprisingly, the villains of the story are not the soldiers and officers who will be her husband's executioners, although the author has not depicted them in a sympathetic light, but rather men generally—her own husband, the carter, who is also a deserter, and all men who leave their wives and cause them to suffer. Highly effective is the twist the author employs, in which a predictable denouement of the plot is avoided and the reader is, frankly, taken by surprise.

On hand as the deserters disembarked from the ship which brought them from the place where the mass desertion took place, Wu-yün Sao was, (she tells her companions on the oxcart) distressed to see that her husband was not among them. Told that he and the other ringleaders were to be sent over in a later shipload, she left to return home:

"I put the child on my back and left the riverbank, with the badge still pinned on, and walked off. My legs were trembling as I walked along. The streets were filled with people who had come over to watch what was happening. I was walking behind the garrison buildings and there at the base of the garrison wall sat the old man with the two packages, but now he only had one package left. I said to him: 'Uncle, didn't your son come either?' The moment I asked him, he arched his back and stuck the ends of his beard in his mouth and chewed on them as he wept.

"He said: 'Since he was one of the ringleaders, capital punishment was carried out on the spot.' At the time I didn't know just what this 'capital punishment' was all about . . . . " (p. 16)

It is a sad story and, even with its flaws, a moving one. The final piece in the collection is "The Family Outsider." It is a long (sixty-five pages) reminiscence of the author's home in Hulan and of her unusual relative, Second Uncle Yu.[23] In this delightful piece Hsiao Hung has recalled more than the sights, sounds, and events of her childhood; she has actually re-created moods. The juvenile language, childish reactions, and points of view of the girl narrator are so believable as to make the people in Hsiao Hung's past as real and as vivid to the reader as they obviously were to the author herself.

The family outsider is Second Uncle Yu, whom we see mainly through the eyes of a child, a child who often teases him, seldom understands him, and only occasionally lets her heart go out to him. There is such honesty in what can be seen of the relationship between this sixty-year-old, illiterate "black sheep" and his seven-year-old niece that the reader finds himself continually drifting back to his own childhood and the people he remembers. As for Second Uncle Yu's even less happy relationships with the author's mother and father, they too are seen through the child's eyes, and the reader is left to interpret them with the "data" provided. It is an engrossing story, one in which the author's effortless recall of illuminating detail makes it truly come alive. There is, for example, the little episode where the girl has sneaked out of her house with a basketful of eggs on which she and the neighbor children plan to feast:

> "Hey, let's divide 'em up. . . so many for each of us, and everybody cooks his own."
> The bonfire blazed up, and the faces of all us kids turned red.
> "O.K., let's cook 'em! Go ahead and put 'em in. . . three apiece. . . . "
> "But there's one left over; who gets that?"
> "Ah, give it to Ya-pa [mute]."
> She took it and went 'Uh, uh.'
> "Quiet down, don't make so much noise! Don't mess up our chance to get somethin' to eat!"
> "Now you got an extra egg. . . so next time don't make those signs at everybody with your hands! Huh? Ya-pa!"
> When the eggshells began turning brown, we were so excited we lost our heads and almost started screaming.
> "Hey! Hey! They're almost done!"
> "Get ready. When I say they're cooked, then hurry. . . . "
> "My egg's bigger than anyone's. . . big as a duck's egg. . . . "
> "Shhh. . . quiet down. Hua's mom is probably awake after all this. . . . "
> (pp. 26–27)

And in the same conspiratorial manner, they finish off their eggs, then lie their way out of trouble. Elsewhere the author writes of the first time the girl caught Second Uncle Yu stealing things from the house, then the second, and the third. . . . With typical cunning and a singular lack of compassion, the little blackmailer works such events into trips to the park and other such advantages. If Second Uncle Yu is an easy mark for children, he does even less well at the hands of his peers, for he is the object of a good deal of rancor and the butt of cruel jokes. One almost wishes he were not so vividly described so that his hapless existence would seem less sad. Even the family cook, knowing that Second Master has an aversion to eating lamb, takes advantage of him:

Once, when it wasn't even mutton soup, but was beef soup, as soon as Second Uncle Yu picked up his spoon, Yang An [the cook] said:
"Mutton soup . . . ."
He put down his spoon, then used his chopsticks to pick up some fried eggplant. Yang An said to him:
"Fried lamb liver and eggplant."
He went over and rinsed off his chopsticks, then went to the cupboard and took out a plate of pickled salted vegetables. Before he got them back to the table, Yang An said:
"Lamb . . . ." He didn't finish.
"What do you mean, lamb?" Second Uncle Yu stood looking at him.
"Lamb . . .lamb . . .um . . .it's, uh, salted vegetables . . .ahh! I mean there's clean salted vegetables, and then there's unclean . . . ."
"What do you mean, unclean?"
"Well, I cut up the vegetables with the knife I use for slicing lamb."
"You can't do that to me! Yang An! . . ." Second Uncle Yu walked away from the table and threw the plate way over on top of it. The table was extremely slippery and the plate crashed and danced on top of it before it bumped into another, and then came to rest. (pp. 62–63)

And so, with all of this, a change comes over Second Uncle Yu:

. . . he started cursing even smaller things; like, for instance, when he stubbed his toe on a piece of brick, he sat on the ground and tightly held the brick down with his hand. It was as though he figured that that piece of brick had moved over in front of his foot on its own. Or if there were birds flying overhead and something dirty landed on his sleeve or somewhere, he would shake it off while he turned his head towards the sky and spoke to the birds that by that time had already flown by:

"You dirty . . .hah! You sure know how to aim, right here on my sleeve. . . what are you, blind? If you have to drop something, then drop it on someone who's wearing silk or satin! Drop it on me and you just waste . . .you bunch of crippled beggars . . . ." (pp. 65–66)

Hsiao Hung, whose feelings of despair are evident in nearly everything else she wrote in Japan, must have taken great pleasure in the writing of "The Family Outsider"; it was perhaps the one respite from frustration and loneliness she had during her months away from Shanghai. This story is the highlight of *On the Oxcart* and one of the most successful works up to this point in her career.

## VI *The Death of Lu Hsün*

At 5:25 A.M. on October 19, 1936, Lu Hsün died in his home at the age of fifty-five. He was buried three days later in the city of Shanghai. On that day literally thousands of people from all walks of life attended his funeral. Hsiao Chün, who had returned to Shanghai less than a week before Lu Hsün's death,[24] was a pallbearer along with Kaji Wataru and ten other young writers. On that same day Hsiao Hung learned that Lu Hsün had died:

Regarding Mr. Chou's death, I had a vague inkling of it from a paper dated the twenty-first, but I couldn't believe that I was right. I ran right over to ask my one and only friend here, who said to me: "You don't understand Japanese; you must have read it wrong." I had high hopes that I was mistaken, and so I returned home with a lighter heart, although earlier on my way over I had been crying.

Last night I was unable to keep from weeping, as I saw a Chinese newspaper in which an unmistakable picture of him was printed, an etching that was simply heartrending. What's most agonizing is that the sound of my weeping cannot blend with the sounds of all of yours. It has now been five days since he left us, and I'm wondering where he is sleeping now."[25]

Hsiao Hung's self-imposed sequestration in Japan had been complete; she was not even corresponding with Lu Hsün. Two weeks before his death, he had written to Shen Ming-fu (Mao Tun): "Since Hsiao Hung left she hasn't written once to me, not even to let me know her address; I heard recently that she was about to return to Shanghai, but I don't know for sure, so I won't be able to pass your information on to her."[26] It takes little imagination to picture the grief that Hsiao Hung must have felt when she learned

that there would be no more letters and no more meetings with her
patron and dear friend. As she wrote to Hsiao Chün a few days later:
"For a man to die is natural, but even knowing the logic in that
statement, emotionally it still doesn't help."[27] Her growing sense of
isolation was unquestionably heightened by Lu Hsün's death.[28]
Characteristically, her thoughts were not only of Lu Hsün, for she
knew how his death would affect his wife and child:

I'm apprehensive about Miss Hsü [Kuang-p'ing] and the sorrow she must
be experiencing. Think of some way to lessen her grief. The best thing to do
is to keep her active and to see her as often as you can; after the initial
period of unbearable grief it will be easier by far for her to get hold of
herself. And then there's the child. I really hate to think of it. I feel like
coming home at once. As I think of that child, now completely alone, how
frightening it is.
   Finally, I want you to send a wreath of flowers or something for me.
Tell Miss Hsü not to cry too much for the sake of the child.[29]

In the years following Lu Hsün's death Hsiao Hung would write
thousands of words to his memory, but she needed only twenty-
three Chinese characters to express her own feelings of personal loss
at the time:

   Precious as a gem, a friend's love;
   One day it is gone;
   The hurt is deeper than from the loss of a gem.[30]

CHAPTER 5

# *"I Am Fated to Walk Alone . . ."*

## Shanghai: 1937

PRECISELY when Hsiao Hung returned to Shanghai is a highly debatable point; in fact, the entire period from mid-October of 1936 until early March of the following year constitutes a biographer's nightmare. By all indications, however, as she wrote in her letter to Hsiao Chün ("I feel like coming home at once"), she returned from Japan within weeks of Lu Hsün's death.[1] By November she had reunited with Hsiao Chün and was living with him on Lü-pan Road (Avenue Dubail) in the French Concession. They soon became very friendly with Kaji Wataru and his wife, Ikeda Yukiko, and reestablished their friendship with Sun Ling and his wife, all of whom were living nearby. According to Sun, Hsiao Hung was by then in high spirits, and it was at about this time that her brother came to visit her in Shanghai.

After her return Hsiao Hung went often both to Hsü Kuang-p'ing's home and to Lu Hsün's grave. On March 8, 1937, she composed a memorial poem to Lu Hsün; with the exception of the two- and three-line verses in "Sand Pebbles," this eulogy, entitled "Pai-mu" (Visit to a Grave), is her only extant poem:

Following behind others,
I entered the graveyard;
Following behind others,
I came to your gravesite.

The day was cloudy and gray;
It was the first time I had paid my respects since you died.

Beside your grave I planted a small floral offering,
But not to call out mournfully to your spirit;
Just to say: "I've come to see you after so long."

75

We trampled on the grass of the graveside path,
While nearby we could hear the sounds of a stone mason carving a
tombstone,
Or a memorial plaque.

At that moment,
In my breast my lungs began to heave.

I weep over you;
My tears are shed not for a man,
But for justice.

With your death
I feel as though justice has gone with you,
Even though justice cannot be taken away by any man.

As we left the graveyard
We were sent off by the sounds of an iron chisel on stone;
I hadn't the courage to ask the stone mason
What sort of memorial plaque he would someday carve for you.[2]

Not spectacular poetry, perhaps, but it is typically Hsiao Hung.

We cannot know what sort of expectations Hsiao Hung carried
back with her from Japan, although if they included a peaceful,
secure life with Hsiao Chün, she was soon to meet with disappointment. His activities after returning to Shanghai are no less
difficult to determine than hers, but we do know that he was becoming more and more active politically and increasingly neglectful
of his common-law wife. Ideologically, he had joined forces with Hu
Feng and several others of Lu Hsün's earlier entourage, and Kaji
Wataru has stated that Hu Feng, Hsiao Chün, Hsiao Hung, and
others had formed their own literary faction with Lu Hsün as their
symbol and self-righteousness as a common trait:

Together with Hu Feng and others they professed on their own initiative to
be members of the "Lu Hsün Faction," and they purposely formed a narrow
relationship for themselves in the contemporary literary circles of Shanghai . . . .Ambitious people like Hu Feng secretly stirred up the situation
and put it to their own advantage in order to shape the influence of their
own sect within the literary circles. Hsiao Chün, who seemed to take great
satisfaction in his reckless brand of anarchism, was motivated to say "only
we understand literature," and I was well able to understand the process by
which he was drawn into that kind of circle.[3]

In sum, Kaji writes that Hsiao Chün was "swept off his feet by Hu Feng."[4] Be that as it may, Hsiao Chün was by this time involved in many leftist activities and had little time for Hsiao Hung. In addition to political activities, there were problems at home; Sun Ling writes: "Their relationship was extremely bad, and when they were together San Lang hit her regularly with his fist, often turning her face black and blue."[5] He also found time to involve himself in some romantic interludes in Shanghai in 1937. Lo Pin-chi recounts with considerable detail (and not a little gusto) an episode involving Hsiao Chün and a well-known editor, "H," and his wife; Hsiao Hung later told a friend of her suspicions in this regard.[6] In short, she was being ignored as well as mistreated, and she no longer had Lu Hsün to turn to. There is evidence that once again in Shanghai she ran away, only to be found by Hsiao Chün's friends and ig-nominiously brought back.[7] And if her private life in 1937 was proving to be as emotionally trying as the previous year, it was an even more barren year in terms of her literary activities. Through-out 1937 she wrote no fiction; her output was limited to the poetry quoted above and perhaps a half dozen personal sketches, all of which appeared in the magazine *Ch'i-yüeh*.[8]

Once again, however, her personal problems were to be eclipsed by a national crisis. On the seventh of July a minor military incident at the Marco Polo Bridge (Lu-kou ch'iao) between Peking and Tientsin touched off the spark that would lead within weeks to the opening of declared hostilities between China and Japan—and eventually to the Second World War. It did not take long for war to reach Shanghai, for on the thirteenth of August the city was attacked—it would fall to the Japanese three months later. Hsiao Hung and Hsiao Chün were indirectly involved in the war at once, for their friends, Kaji Wataru and his wife, openly advocated Chinese resistance to the Japanese aggressors and were now being hunted as collaborators by the Japanese. They were taken in by Hsiao Hung and Hsiao Chün until a more permanent but equally safe location could be found. With Hsiao Hung's help, they found refuge elsewhere in the city, and she continued to see to their needs.[9] Eventually the Kajis fled to the interior, and it soon became evident to most writers that to remain in Shanghai would be both undesirable and dangerous. Just when Hsiao Hung and the others left cannot be stated precisely, though it was probably during September, or perhaps early October; they travelled to the twin cities of Wuchang and Hankow (Wuhan) in Hupei.[10]

## I  *Hupei, Shansi and Shensi (1937–1938)*

With the fall of Shanghai in November, there were several options open to Chinese writers there: some, like Lu Hsün's brother, Chou Tso-jen, remained in Japanese-occupied territory where they continued to write in relative freedom (the limitations are obvious); they could go to the Communist stronghold of Yenan and join such writers as Ting Ling; or they could leave for Nationalist-controlled areas, primarily Wuhan, Chungking, and Kweilin. Initially, Wuhan became the new center of literary activities in the Nationalist-controlled areas, and a new organization, the Chinese Writers' Anti-Aggression Association, was founded on March 27, 1938, in Hankow, with branches in other cities. This association was far and away the most important, the most active, and the broadest-based organization of its kind in wartime China. In line with the proclamations of détente between the Nationalists and the Communists in order to promote a unified resistance to the Japanese, support for the organization came from all sectors, and patriotic propaganda was the order of the day. Just what Hsiao Hung's relationship to the organization was is not clear, although the little writing she did publish in Wuhan bespeaks a somewhat half-hearted attempt to write in accordance with the Association's policy of strident wartime propaganda. Throughout the remainder of 1937 and much of the following year her writings appeared only in *Ch'i-yüeh*, which published primarily those writers in the circle around Hu Feng.

In Wuhan, Hsiao Hung and Hsiao Chün lived in the home of the poet Chiang Hsi-chin in Wuchang, across the Yangtze River from Hankow, where the *Ch'i-yüeh* Society had its offices.[11] Chiang's home must have served as a boardinghouse of sorts, for other writers stayed with him during that time, including the Northeastern writer, Tuan-mu Hung-liang.[12] Mei Lin, whom Hsiao Hung and Hsiao Chün met again in Wuchang, has described Tuan-mu Hung-liang in a brief but revealing reference:

Once a man with long sideburns and a pale face, slightly hunch-backed, with a hoarse voice, and wearing a faddish suit with padded shoulders, walked in; he removed a pair of brown soft leather gloves from his thin and delicate hands. . . . [13]

Stark contrast to Hsiao Chün!

By the time Hsiao Hung and Hsiao Chün arrived in Wuchang, their relationship once again seemed no longer sustainable. The relish with which he continued to expose her weaknesses to their friends and the physical abuse that occasionally forced her to seek refuge in the homes of friends continued to torment her in Wuchang.[14] In former days, when the situation reached an intolerable stage, her only recourse had been to flee, but this time there was an added element—Hsiao Hung had found an admirer and prospective protector. Tuan-mu Hung-liang was showing interest in her as a woman, and since she was the better-known writer of the two, she was placed in the unaccustomed role of the superior in their relationship. Most importantly, perhaps, Tuan-mu Hung-liang was not one of Hsiao Chün's "cronies," so for the first time Hsiao Hung no longer had to feel that she was being watched by him. Consequently, Tuan-mu Hung-liang became the third member of a short-lived romantic triangle.

Such an atmosphere did not bode well for creativity, and none of the threesome did much writing throughout the remainder of the year and the first few months of 1938. All were involved with Hu Feng's *Ch'i-yüeh* Society, and each contributed a few pieces of reportage, but they were mainly involved in trying to define just what their mission as writers should be. Such discussions would take on increased importance as the Chinese Writers' Anti-Aggression Association began its advocacy of writer participation in village and army life. One such discussion took place in mid-January in Hankow, presided over by Hu Feng and attended by ten writers, Hsiao Hung and Tuan-mu Hung-liang among them (Hsiao Chün pleaded illness and did not attend). The meeting, a record of which appeared in *Ch'i-yüeh*, is of interest to us because of the opinions expressed by Hsiao Hung, opinions which were generally contrary to the trend of more active participation in the front lines by writers. Complaints were being voiced by other participants who felt that by remaining in the city they were separating themselves from the people and from "life." They found themselves out of touch and unable to write, and their answer was to immerse themselves in the struggle which they assumed would lead to the inspiration to write. Although some of her comments at this forum bespeak a lack of sophistication in matters of theory, Hsiao Hung nevertheless effectively debunks the belief that front lines produce the only real wartime literature:

As I see it, we aren't cut off from life at all. For example, taking refuge during an air-raid alert is a part of wartime living conditions. The problem is that we haven't grasped its significance. Even if we were at the front lines where people were being killed by Japanese soldiers, if we hadn't grasped its significance, we still couldn't write of it.[15]

What she is saying, of course, is that there is material all around, and that it is not a paucity of material that contributes to a writer's inability to produce (a convenient excuse, but hardly a reason) as much as a flaw in his attitude or insufficient observation and understanding, and that with such a flaw even major events will lose their significance for a writer.

But many writers were touched by the appeal to participate in the more spectacular aspects of the war. In January a call went out from Li Kung-p'u (1901–1946), the founder and director of the People's Revolutionary University (Min-tsu ko-ming ta-hsüeh), located in Lin-fen, Shansi Province, for people from many fields to come and aid the struggle by teaching. Hsiao Chün decided to go, and Hsiao Hung, who was still living with him, would accompany him there, perhaps in part because Tuan-mu Hung-liang was also making plans to leave for Shansi.

The group left together on one of the last days of January and travelled to Lin-fen. There Hsiao Hung met for the first time the woman with whom Lu Hsün had compared her, Ting Ling, who, with her Northwest Battlefield Service Troupe, had arrived in Lin-fen in October of the previous year from Yenan.[16] She was immediately taken with Hsiao Hung, having seen something in the younger woman that reminded her of her own pre-war days,[17] and they became friends.

Toward the end of February Japanese airplanes began to bomb the city of Lin-fen preparatory to a land invasion of the area, and so, less than a month after their arrival, the group made plans to leave; the university was leaving en masse for Yenan. Hsiao Chün, who was being asked to accompany the students, was again giving thought to exchanging his pen for a rifle,[18] and he decided not to remain with his friends, but to travel alone to northern Shansi and investigate the resistance efforts there. Whether or not his and Hsiao Hung's worsening relationship and the presence of Tuan-mu Hung-liang contributed to this decision can only be guessed. He has written in considerable detail about the events surrounding his and Hsiao Hung's separation in Lin-fen, and although much of it sounds highly self-serving, it is the most comprehensive account available.

According to him, Hsiao Hung was incensed by his decision to join the resistance fighters and reminded him that at his age and with his "writing talents," he was too important to sacrifice himself.[19] He recalls that she was reduced to tears of despair and begged him not to leave:

"I don't want to go to Yün-ch'eng; I want to go into town [Lin-fen] with you . . . we'll live or die together! Together . . . otherwise, let's leave together; I won't have a peaceful moment if you stay behind alone, because I know your temperament."[20]

This one excerpt should serve to show the general tenor of his recollections. He asked Ting Ling to watch over Hsiao Hung and take her to the city of Sian in Shensi. To their friends, all of whom were well aware of Hsiao Chün's mercurial nature and unshakable self-esteem, the separation seemed to be a temporary thing. The three principals in this triangular relationship, however, knew better, and just prior to the departure of Ting Ling's train, Hsiao Chün confided in Nieh Kan-nu that the situation was much more serious than it seemed:

"I am in better physical condition than the rest of you. I can stand up under hardships, and I can join the fight. I'm going to Wu-t'ai [in northern Shansi], but don't tell Hsiao Hung."
"What will she do then?"
"Well, she thinks most highly of you, so you look after her. In worldly matters she's a babe in the woods, and she's easily taken advantage of."
"Then, later the two of you will . . . ."
"She is simple, pure and honest, stubborn and talented; I love her, but she isn't a wife, at least she isn't mine."
"What! You mean you two are . . . ."
"Don't be so surprised. As I said, I love her; I would even be willing to meet her halfway. This is a painful situation, painful for her too. But if she hadn't brought up the subject of separation, we would remain husband and wife indefinitely, for I would never abandon her first."[21]

Several interesting points emerge from this exchange: first, Hsiao Chün's insufferable boastings of his own strength and durability and condescending remarks concerning Hsiao Hung, qualities which contributed substantially to her alienation from him, are evident right up to the end. He is undeniably correct in his evaluation of her vulnerability, but he has neglected to consider that he was, to a large extent, the cause of it. As for his feelings for her, they were probably genuine, though incredibly limited. In her role as common-law wife, she had been a combination of protected child, homemaker, and all-around factotum. Had she been a stronger woman under such circumstances (a woman more like Ting Ling, for instance), the relationship would probably not have lasted as long as it did, or, at the very least, would not have taken the form it had. After their separation, Hsiao Hung made her feelings along this line clear to Nieh Kan-nu:

"I love Hsiao Chün—even now. He is an excellent writer and an ideological comrade; besides, we have struggled against hardships together. But being his wife entails too much suffering. I don't know why you men have such tempers, why you want to make your wives the targets of your outbursts, and why you aren't honest with them. . . . I've endured unjustified shame too long already . . . ."[22]

The final sentence in Hsiao Chün's earlier comment is important; it was she who had ended their common-law marriage, not he. After all, he had fared quite well from the union, for Hsiao Hung had served him for several years as servant, mistress, alter ego, and "whipping boy"; he would have been loathe to bring their relationship to an end. As for her, it is by no means surprising that she was unhappy in her role, but her past indecisiveness and increasingly dependent nature would, on the face of it, have made carrying out such a decision seem unlikely. The answer, obviously, is Tuan-mu Hung-liang. We need look no further for evidence of Tuan-mu Hung-liang's role in the dissolution of the relationship than Hsiao Chün's own writings. His belittling and abusive comments concerning Tuan-mu Hung-liang and occasional flights of self-delusion are clear indication of his realization that Tuan-mu Hung-liang had successfully undermined his position.

When he [Tuan-mu Hung-liang] spoke, his voice had a shrill quality, like the sound of a duck. That sound was in perfect harmony with his pushed-in nose, his thin lips that were pursed in the shape of a sack, and his dark coloring. I hadn't talked with him for several days, because I despise people like him who always put on airs that they are learned "major writers," and who delight in building their own good fortune at the expense of others! I detest him. I detest all pitiful things (tung-hsi) like him.[23]

. . . I was being swept away by my swirling emotions:
—I should go along with her to Yün-ch'eng. If I send her off alone, she'll be so concerned about me that she'll never have a moment's peace; she doesn't have much in common with the tall "R" [?] and the others, and as for "T" [Tuan-mu Hung-liang] with his pushed-in nose, she despises him even more than I do.[24]

And so, their protestations of mutual love notwithstanding, Hsiao Hung and Hsiao Chün separated, and though there would be one more brief encounter a few weeks later, the union had been dissolved after a stormy five and a half-years. In many respects it had been an unlikely and unwise match from the beginning, one which in some regards had benefitted them both, but its unpleasant aspects had much more serious and lasting-effects on her than on him. Hsiao Hung's desire for a peaceful and secure existence was constantly frustrated, not only by the difficult times during which they were together, but also by Hsiao Chün's lack of understanding and by his overbearing attitude. On the other hand, it seems evident that her career as a writer began largely under his influence and encouragement, and it is difficult to imagine her striking out on her own in furtherance of her career. Thus her rise to prominence owed as much to Hsiao Chün as it did, for example, to Lu Hsün. But, all things considered, it was a relationship which had reached its logical end. The transition for Hsiao Hung was a relatively smooth one, for Tuan-mu Hung-liang was waiting anxiously in the wings. But if she expected her situation to improve markedly, she was headed for even greater disappointment.

On about the twenty-fifth of February, Ting Ling's dramatic troupe and her new travelling companions boarded a train for the south. On the first of March they crossed the Yellow River at T'ung-kuan Pass on the Shansi-Shensi border[25] and a few days later arrived in Sian. They had left just in time, for the Japanese soon swept through Lin-fen and occupied territory on the northern bank of the Yellow River, no more than one hundred miles from Sian. But for Hsiao Hung, personal problems remained uppermost in her mind; she had terminated her relationship with Hsiao Chün but wasn't completely convinced it had been the right thing to do, and she was forming a new liaison with a man whom she didn't particularly like personally, let alone love. According to Nieh Kan-nu, she often complained that Tuan-mu Hung-liang was "a coward, a sycophant, and a horse's ass who spends all his time acting pompous."[26] But Hsiao Hung's dissatisfaction was not limited to her relationship with Tuan-mu Hung-liang; her view of the world, particularly the woman's world, was turning increasingly sour:

"I am a woman. The canopy of heaven over the heads of women is low, while our wings are flimsy and our burdens heavy and unpleasant! What's even worse is that women are excessively self-sacrificing, not out of courage but out of cowardice. A state of inertia develops in us after living a long time with no one to aid us, and under conditions that require us to be sacrificing, so that we accept sacrifice willingly. I know that, but still I can't help thinking: Just what am I in this world? What is scorn to me? What does disaster mean to me? For that matter, what is death to me? I don't know. Am I, after all, one person, or am I two people? Should I be thinking like this? Or like that? You're right, I want to fly, but still I have the feeling . . . that I'll come crashing down."[27]

The final reference is to the words of the Russian poet Vasilij Eroshenko (1899–1952), "Don't look down, for that is where the enslaved meet their end."[28] Nieh Kan-nu was urging her to fly upwards, referring to her burgeoning and, to him, undesirable relationship with Tuan-mu Hung-liang. It is obvious that by this time Hsiao Hung's predominant mood was one of self-pity, and she exhibited marked symptoms of paranoia. In a life in which there had been no dearth of emotional crises, this period certainly was one of the most trying she had yet experienced. She later told a friend how good her home in Hulan seemed to her then,[29] although returning was out of the question for obvious reasons.

Not long after their arrival in Sian, Ting Ling and Nieh Kan-nu decided to go to Yenan. Hsiao Hung was encouraged by both of them to go along, but she declined. Nieh, who seemed to be trying very hard to prevent her from getting involved with Tuan-mu Hung-liang, even brought up the prospect of meeting Hsiao Chün there, but still she demurred. The following day they left (not before Nieh had made another silent reference to his flight metaphor), and Hsiao Hung remained behind accompanied by Tuan-mu Hung-liang. Two weeks later Ting Ling and Nieh returned to Sian with Hsiao Chün in tow—they had met in Yenan—where they were confronted with the sight of Hsiao Hung and Tuan-mu Hung-liang emerging together from Ting Ling's room in the school where the dramatic troupe was quartered; the embarrassment which followed touched them all. Nieh's recollections of ensuing events are of interest:

D.M. [Tuan-mu Hung-liang] hurriedly came over [to Nieh's room], picked up a brush and began dusting my clothes off. With his head lowered, he said, "Rough times!" But what I heard was, "If anything happens, you have to stand by me!" I could tell; it was clearer than if I had seen it all for myself: that golden-winged fabulous bird, hampered by her own spirit of self-sacrifice, had somersaulted in the air and was plunging down to the place "where the enslaved meet their end."[30]

There were evidently a few aborted attempts by Hsiao Chün to talk the situation out with her; then finally she and Tuan-mu Hung-liang left Sian (in April) and returned together to Wuchang, to the very same room that she had earlier shared with Hsiao Chün.[31] Hsiao Chün subsequently went to Chengtu in Szechuan Province, where he wrote the record of his travels in the interior from which we have seen excerpts; then he returned to Yenan, where he was welcomed enthusiastically as a major literary figure.[32] While in Sian, Hsiao Hung had again been singularly unproductive as a writer, her sole contribution consisting of a joint effort with Tuan-mu Hung-liang, Nieh Kan-nu, and Sai K'o to produce, at Ting Ling's request, a propaganda play entitled *T'u-chi (The Blitz).*[33]

The reception she received from her friends in Wuhan, people who were for the most part Hsiao Chün's friends also, was decidedly cool. She was immediately put on the defensive. Her reaction to a well-meaning bit of advice by the unidentified "S" is typical:

"Your friends don't oppose your break with Hsiao Chün, but can't you be independent and live alone?"
"Why is it that I have to live alone? Because I'm a woman?" Then Hsiao Hung said: "I don't give a damn about the opinions of my friends. I can't live in accordance with the ideals of my friends . . . I have my own ways!"[34]

Hsiao Hung's self-created isolation from others was clearly increasing.

Besides Mei Lin, who had little contact with Hsiao Hung in Wuhan, there were a few other old friends whom she could see: Shu Ch'ün and Lo Feng had begun publishing a semimonthly magazine entitled *Chan-ti*, while Sun Ling was living across the river in Hankow. Sun seems to be the only one who saw much of Hsiao

Hung, and then only when she found herself in difficulties. For by that time she was again pregnant, although just whose child it was is a disputed point and need not concern us here. And more trouble was not long in coming. In the summer of 1938 the Japanese turned their attention to the cities of Wuchang and Hankow, and the situation there became critical. Tuan-mu Hung-liang had hopes of becoming a war correspondent, but was unsuccessful in landing the job, so toward the end of July he made plans to leave for Szechuan. In August he, Mei Lin, and Lo Feng boarded a Yangtze River boat for Chungking. As Mei Lin tells it, Hsiao Hung was left behind to take a delayed steamer, ostensibly for her convenience.[35] But Sun Ling recalls that she had been more or less abandoned by Tuan-mu Hung-liang; seemingly, he had tired of her already.[36] During her final month in Hankow—she had crossed over from Wuchang after Tuan-mu Hung-liang's departure—she wrote a short piece for the *Ta-kung pao* entitled "Fen-ho ti yüan-yüeh" (The Moon Over the Fen River), which, in just over one thousand words, tells of an elderly blind woman whose son had died in the army and whose daughter-in-law had left home leaving a small daughter in her care. The old woman loses her mind, and the story ends with her sitting next to the Fen River (which runs past Lin-fen) in the moonlight, the faint sounds of a performance by a patriotic troupe of actors in the air. The author's despondency is manifestly clear in this piece.

## II  *Chungking: 1938–1939*

In September, the ninth month of Hsiao Hung's pregnancy, she left Wuhan for Chungking. En route, at Yi-ch'ang (in Hupei), she fell on a pier and lay there a long time without being able to get up, until she was eventually aided by a boatman.[37] By mid-month she had arrived in Chungking. Where she lived during her first few months in the city is not known, though at some time during that period she was delivered of a dead infant. Her mood upon arrival was understandably bleak, and there must have been anger in her voice when she met Mei Lin, one of those who had left her behind in Wuhan, and said to him:

"I am always walking alone; before, in the Northeast, then when I went to Japan after I had come to Shanghai, and my subsequent return from Japan, and now coming to Chungking, I have always walked my road alone. It's as though I am fated to walk alone. . . ."[38]

In late December her old friend Ikeda Yukiko arrived in Chungking (from Kweilin) and moved into a house in the suburb of Ko-lo-shan. Hsiao Hung moved into Ikeda's home where she spent the spring of 1939, a period during which she regained her health to some degree and even her spirits. There she met another Japanese woman, Midorigawa Eiko.[39] Midorigawa remembers Hsiao Hung then as being fond of smoking, drinking, singing, and chatting at length, primarily with Ikeda,[40] who was perhaps her closest female friend.[41] Then too, for the first time in a long while she was busy writing; at least four sketches included in her next prose collection are dated in the early spring of that year at Ko-lo-shan.

During this time Tuan-mu Hung-liang was teaching at Fu-tan University along with the writer Chin Yi, and before the end of spring he and Hsiao Hung were back together, living in a small set of rooms in the Chungking suburb of Pei-p'ei where Fu-tan University was temporarily located. Again, past and future events cast doubt on the wisdom of a reconciliation on Hsiao Hung's part, although her peculiar brand of tunnel-vision lends the choice a degree of inevitability. Pei-p'ei, as one of the most scenic spots in the Chungking area, was particularly conducive to writing, and the ensuing year there would be one of the most productive periods of writing in her life. She wrote several sketches and short stories, plus her long memorial to Lu Hsün, *A Remembrance of Lu Hsün hsiensheng,* all of which we shall momentarily examine. It was in Chungking too that she completed a first draft of her autobiographical novel, *Tales of Hulan River.*[42]

Not surprisingly, on the personal level things had not improved much for her; the physical abuse she had suffered at the hands of Hsiao Chün had been replaced by constant belittling and emotional abuse at the hands of Tuan-mu Hung-liang.[43] Chin Yi has recounted one typical incident in which Tuan-mu Hung-liang, whom he characterizes as a selfish, affected sloth, openly disparaged Hsiao Hung's writings in his presence. Among her other duties as Tuan-mu Hung-liang's common-law wife she also hand-copied his novel *Ta-chiang (The Great River),* which he completed in Pei-p'ei, and in Chin Yi's words: "He treated women as though they were men's private chattels."[44] It has a familiar ring!

Hsiao Hung's arrival in Chungking signalled her return to a writing schedule which was to prove as productive as the two years prior to her departure for Japan. In all, she completed at least six short

stories, which were subsequently published in book form by the
Shanghai Magazine Company.[45]

### III    A Cry in the Wilderness

*A Cry in the Wilderness* marks a general improvement over earlier attempts in Hsiao Hung's handling of short stories, although the
selections still lack the qualities that would establish her as a first-
rate short story writer. The title piece, one of three fairly long
stories in the collection, is perhaps the most politically oriented, and
it is a weak story, partly because of its length. The author's talents
for capturing details and for painting scenes that are so effective in
her personal reminiscences tend occasionally to weigh heavily in her
fiction. Unable to sustain the reader's interest from page to page
because of what can only be considered excessive padding, a sopor-
ific pace is the result, and the few highlights of the story are of
insufficient intensity to recapture the reader's interest—climaxes go
unnoticed.

Set in Manchuria near the Sungari River, "A Cry in The Wilderness" begins by portraying an elderly couple whose son has not
returned home for several days. The father, Uncle Ch'en, afraid that
the youth has joined the militia, is unable to conduct his normal
routine due to anxieties over his son's well-being, and his distress
and edginess are often neatly captured in the narration. One of the
highlights of the story is the longish episode of Auntie Ch'en's decision to pray and make sacrifices at the long-neglected family altar.
She forgets not only how to arrange the paraphernalia, but even the
traditional words of prayer. Flustered, she merely says what is in
her heart and is so moved by her own words that she cannot continue. Eventually the son returns home with the story that he has
been out hunting. But his absences from home increase, and the
truth emerges that he has been hired as a bridge construction la-
borer for the Japanese. Relieved that his son has not recklessly
joined the resistance, and proud that he is now a wage-earner,
Uncle Ch'en quickly makes sure that his far-sighted, considerate,
and capable son becomes the talk of the village. But then the reader
is let in on the secret that the son is, in fact, involved with the
resistance movement and is making plans to sabotage the bridge.
Before long, on a day in which Uncle Ch'en is in one of his most
ebullient moods, a villager comes to report that a train has been
sabotaged and derailed and that all the laborers have been arrested.

In a blinding windstorm—a repeat of the opening pages—the old man, on the verge of madness, sets out alone in search of his son. There is potential in this story, although it is too long and, as is too often the case with Hsiao Hung, the forced and almost anticlimactic ending is a letdown. At once transparently obvious and much too sketchy, the denouement further weakens an already mediocre story.

The least typical story in the collection is "T'ao-nan" (Flight from Danger). A new type of character appears in this short piece, a man who is both comical and hypocritical—in these respects not at all unlike Second Uncle Yu. But Ho Nan-sheng is a satirical character, a schoolteacher who is in possession of a fat and easily intimidated wife, a houseful of junk, and several eccentricities and firm convictions regarding people and events.

Just what was that defect of his? Well, whenever he was about to find himself in a difficult situation, even if the situation never materialized, the minute he began to contemplate something unpleasant happening to him in the future he at once grew dissatisfied with the whole world. Situations like, for instance, after he took off his socks at night, they fell to the floor, where they were nearly chewed up by a mouse; or, on his way down from the lectern he stepped on a piece of chalk, nearly falling down as the chalk rolled under his foot. In a word, if the danger failed to materialize, and nothing at all came of the matter, for him the thought of what might have happened disturbed him unbelievably. So besides his penchant for saying what he thought about the Chinese, there was another sentence he habitually uttered, and that was:

"When the time comes, then what'll we do. . . ." (p. 56)

Ho makes plans to flee the city—it is wartime—all the while telling his class that he would be the last person to flee. With consummate duplicity, he begins by saying that "in four or five days he would be back—actually, once he left, he was gone for good—and ended by declaring that the final victory belonged to our side; other than that, he told them that his fate was tied up with that of Shensi—they would live or die together—and that he would never flee."(p. 59)

Finally the day comes, and there he is at the train station with great quantities of useless junk, all of which fits neatly into his plan for survival. But in the confusion the first two trains leave without him and his family. The next day they are on the train and arrive at a friend's home as the story ends. With uncharacteristic humor and satire, and a character type that is almost unique in the entire corpus of Hsiao Hung's writings, "Flight from Danger" is a well-devised and enjoyable story, revealing a new aspect of her literary talent. The story's effectiveness belies her total lack of experience in the area of satire, and it provides an enjoyable diversion from the prevailing mood in fiction of the early war years, both in general terms and with Hsiao Hung specifically.

The shortest story in the collection "Hai-tzu ti chiang-yen" (The Child's Speech) is a somewhat touching though largely unsubstantial piece concerning a child called upon to give an impromptu speech at a revolutionary school, and who mistakes as mockery the delighted response his immature patriotic words elicit from his listeners. The final three stories, "Shan hsia" (At the Foot of the Mountain), "Meng-lung ti ch'i-tai" (Vague Expectations), and "Lien-hua ch'ih" (The Lotus Pond), are all very much in the typical Hsiao Hung mold. All are essentially psychological or emotional portraits of peasants, all are reminiscent of earlier stories, and at least two, if not wholly successful, have bright spots.

In "The Lotus Pond," a sickly boy whose father has died and whose mother has remarried, is left in the care of his grandfather. Unable to support his grandson, the old man becomes a professional grave-robber. The descriptions of the amulets the old man carries to ward off the evils he fears he may encounter and of the booty he collects and his means of disposing of it, provide the only redeeming features of the story. Generally weak and overly melodramatic, "The Lotus Pond" is seriously weakened by the forced, almost gratuitous anti-Japanese episode in which the desperate old man makes contact with the local Japanese garrison (from grave-robber to traitor!); he is subsequently scorned and driven away by the Japanese, and his grandson is physically maltreated, an event that ultimately leads to the boy's death. The entire episode, which it must be assumed is the story's *raison d'etre,* and which occupies but four out of a total of forty pages, is disorganized and organically unrelated to the main body of the story.

On the other hand, "Vague Expectations," though reminiscent of many of the author's earlier stories, ends on a note of guarded optimism. The heroine, Li-ma, is a twenty-five-year-old, healthy, attractive, and innocent servant who has hopes of marrying one of her employer's military bodyguards. Prior to going off to the front lines, the young man pays one last visit to the wife of his employer.

While he is talking with the older woman, Li-ma runs out to buy him cigarettes, and when she returns he has already departed; she is left only with memories and promises. But for once Hsiao Hung does not end the story on a sad note. Whether politically or emotionally motivated, she extends a ray of hope:

> That evening she dreamt that Chin Li-chih had returned from the front lines. "I've come back to set up a home for us; from today on everything will be fine." They had won the war.
> What's more, Chin Li-chih's hair was as black as it had been before.
> He said: "We had to win; how could we have lost? It doesn't make any sense!"
> Li-ma had a gentle smile on her face as she dreamt. (p. 13)

The final story, "At the Foot of the Mountain," is among the author's slowest-moving short stories, though there appears in it one truly suspenseful episode. Burdened with entirely too much descriptive material, it begins laboriously by setting a scene that could have been rendered more economically. The story is of a destitute and crippled woman who lives alone with her daughter on the banks of the Yangtze River. The uncomplaining and industrious child, the reader discovers nearly halfway through the story, has recently begun working in the home of a well-to-do family, and life takes a pleasant turn for the two of them. All goes well until the girl's wages are cut from four *yüan* to two, and several envious neighbors begin to encourage the mother to ask that the original sum be reinstated. Mother Lin spends several agonizing hours weighing the pros and cons of such an action, until finally one day she goes to confront her daughter's employer; the results are disastrous, as the girl is fired, and she and her mother once again are without an income. "At the Foot of the Mountain" is the story of a good woman who injudiciously heeds the advice of others whose motives are not in her best interest, and of the tragedy and regret that follow; the parallels with Hsiao Hung herself are striking.

## IV   A Remembrance of Lu Hsün hsien-sheng

Lu Hsün hsien-sheng's laugh was bright and clear—it came from his heart. Whenever someone said something funny, Lu Hsün hsien-sheng would laugh so hard he couldn't even hold a cigarette, often laughing so hard he began to cough.

X          X

Lu Hsün hsien-sheng walked with a light, brisk step; my clearest memory is seeing him put his hat on his head, stretch out his left foot, and walk out the door without a thought for anything else.

X          X

Lu Hsün hsien-sheng didn't pay much attention to what others were wearing; he would say: "I don't even notice the clothes that other people have on . . . ."

Once, when he was just getting over an illness, Lu Hsün hsien-sheng was sitting in his reclining chair, smoking next to an open window, and I was there in an outlandish bright red blouse with wide sleeves.

I asked: "Chou hsien-sheng, how do my clothes look?"

Lu Hsün hsien-sheng took a quick look from head to toe: "Not very good."

After a moment he added: "You're wearing the wrong color skirt. It's not that the blouse isn't good looking—all colors are good looking—but with a red blouse you should wear a red skirt, or else a black one, but brown is no good. Put those two colors together and you have a mismatch. Haven't you ever watched a foreigner out walking? You'll never see one of them wearing a green skirt with a purple blouse, or a white blouse over a red skirt . . . ."[46]

So begins Hsiao Hung's long and intensely personal memorial to Lu Hsün. In A Remembrance of Lu Hsün hsien-sheng she has captured the essence of his life in Shanghai during his final years as only an observant writer and intimate friend could have done. She makes no attempt to delve into the workings of his mind or to discuss his political activities, influence, position, or weaknesses and vulnerability. She has, rather, opened up the doors of his home and given the reader a rare glimpse of his daily life, his family, the physical objects that decorated the house, and, most unforgettably, some of his personal traits and eccentricities. She has combined the artist's knack for bringing objects and events to life with her distinctively feminine style of writing to produce what is often considered the most memorable and penetrating portrait of Lu Hsün to date.

A Remembrance of Lu Hsün hsien-sheng was first published in book form in July, 1940, by the Sheng-huo Book Company; an Afterword by the author is dated October 26, 1939.[47] Inasmuch as Hsiao Hung's work is but fifty-five pages long, one related piece each by Hsü Shou-shang and Hsü Kuang-p'ing have been appended. This was not Hsiao Hung's first memorial to Lu Hsün, as we have seen, nor was it to be her last;[48] it is, however, her finest. Parts of the work had appeared elsewhere prior to its being published in book form, including approximately one-third (with the order of entries altered somewhat) in the December, 1939, issue of *Wen-hsüeh chi-lin* under the name "Lu Hsün hsien-sheng sheng-huo yi-lüeh" (Brief Recollections of Lu Hsün's Life).[49]

The range of observations in *A Remembrance of Lu Hsün hsien-sheng* is broad indeed. Every room in the house is described in meticulous detail, as are Lu Hsün's desk, bookcases, and virtually everything that was important to him. As for people who appear under Hsiao Hung's microscope, there are Lu Hsün, his child, his brother, Chou Chien-jen, his doctor, even the servants who worked in his home, and, of course, his wife, Hsü Kuang-p'ing. Center stage, obviously, is Lu Hsün himself. Few of his habits and preferences have escaped notice, whether it be his choice in beverage (green tea), his favorite means of relaxation (reading), or his pet peeve (illegibly written letters). Perhaps of greatest interest to the reader are the schedule Lu Hsün followed and the pace he set for himself. Hsiao Hung has recorded both:

Lu Hsün hsien-sheng began entertaining guests from two or three o'clock in the afternoon until five or six, and if the guests were staying for dinner, afterwards they would have tea with him. . . .

By the time the guests had left it was already after midnight, the time that most people would be ready for bed; but for Lu Hsün hsien-sheng it was time to start to work. Before he actually began he rested his eyes for a moment, lit a cigarette, and lay down on his bed; before he had finished his cigarette, Hsü [Kuang-p'ing] hsien-sheng was probably already asleep. (How could Hsü hsien-sheng fall asleep so quickly? Because at six or seven o'clock the next morning she had to be up to begin her household chores.) By this time Hai-ying was in his room on the third floor sleeping with his nanny.

The house would be completely quiet, and outside his window as well; Lu Hsün hsien-sheng would get up, sit at his writing desk, and begin to write beneath his green lamp.

Hsü hsien-sheng used to say that when the roosters crowed in the morning Lu Hsün hsien-sheng would still be sitting there—the horns of cars outside had started up, and Lu Hsün hsien-sheng was still sitting there.

Sometimes Hsü hsien-sheng would awaken and see the bright light streaming in through the window; the light from the lamp would be subdued, and Lu Hsün hsien-sheng's silhouette would be gray as he continued to sit there.

Everyone else would be getting up, and then Lu Hsün hsien-sheng would go to bed. (p. 19)

Interesting, and in some places engrossing, as Hsiao Hung's narrative is, *A Remembrance of Lu Hsün hsien-sheng* is too long by about half, and it often tends to drag. Some of the material is of little or no interest, and one questions the wisdom of its inclusion. Certainly such information as the fact that Lu Hsün wrapped his own parcels and was not satisfied unless they were both neat and symmetrical is of little concern to most readers. Unwittingly, she has also occasionally shown her subjects in a less than favorable light. In some places Lu Hsün emerges as a cantankerous and monumentally stubborn man, as well as a very caustic one. Hsiao Hung's scrupulous honesty and attention to detail also from time to time work to the disadvantage of Lu Hsün's immediate family, to the point that the long-suffering Hsü Kuang-p'ing's personality seems little more than an extension of her husband's, and their child emerges as an insufferably spoiled brat who seems immature for his years.

But, in the final pages, the chronicle of Lu Hsün's last days, the author, who was away during the time, makes no attempt to pad her account with undue drama or lamentation and, as a result, gives her work a dignified and moving ending:

October 17, 1936, Lu Hsün hsien-sheng's illness returned; it was asthma again.
The 17th, a sleepless night.
The 18th, an entire day of gasping.
The 19th, early morning, he was failing rapidly. Right before dawn, just like any other day, his work finished, he rested. (p. 55)

One month before the publication of *A Remembrance of Lu Hsün hsien-sheng*, in June, 1940, Ta shih-tai Book Company published a collection of seventeen pieces of prose under the title of *Prose Writings of Hsiao Hung*. The first nine pieces were taken from *The Bridge* (four with changed titles); of the remainder, those concerning Lu Hsün, Ikeda Yukiko, and Hsiao Hung's recollections of her school years have already been mentioned. We shall presently see an excerpt of yet another piece, "Fang-huo-che" (The Arsonists). The final three pieces, all written in Ko-lo-shan, are about a nearby Buddhist monastery, a young refugee, and the chair-bearers on the

Yangtze River. In the last piece, "Hua-kan" (Polished Sedan-Poles), the author has very deftly compared the lives of the wretchedly poor and overworked men with the mules that accompany them on the banks of the Yangtze. Again, as an observant artist, she has captured sights and sounds that often escape others.

At least one more of Hsiao Hung's stories was published during her stay in Chungking, though when it was written is not known. "Huang-ho" (The Yellow River) appeared in the magazine *Wen-yi chen-ti* (II, No. 8) shortly after Hsiao Hung's arrival in Chungking and may very well date from her days in Wuhan, or even Sian. It is a typically low-key story, in which the hero's reminiscences form the gist of the tale. It is about a boatman who plies the Yellow River at the T'ung-kuan Pass on the Shensi-Shansi border, and who ferries a soldier from the Eighth Route Army across to Shansi. He recounts the highlights of his life, mostly tragic, and ends by asking the soldier what the fate of the common people will be after victory in the War of Resistance. The soldier replies: "This time victory will be ours . . . life will be good again for the common people."[50]

But before they would be witness to victory in the war the common people were in for some more suffering. On May 1, 1939, waves of Japanese airplanes first emerged from the mist which enveloped the poorly defended city of Chungking, the wartime capital of the Nationalist government. Over the next two months the city was subjected to a merciless pounding by the Japanese airforce, and many areas were severely damaged, not to mention the grievous loss of life. Hsiao Hung was witness to this tragedy and later wrote about it in near-hysterical terms in "The Arsonists":

Before the air of this burned out area had cleared, when the tiles were still hot enough to scald your hand, the Japanese arsonists sitting in their airplanes were coming over again; it was the 12th of May.

The air-raid sirens were sounding everywhere. Whether in the main streets or far into the lanes, those within hearing and those not, those who had made preparations and those who remained oblivious—all were caught up in the waves of sound.

That shattered wall that simply wouldn't fall was abandoned. The people who were strolling along the streets just a moment before were thrown into a panic . . . had gone mad, and began running and gasping; some were dragging children along, some were dragging women along, and the faces of others had lost their color. The streets gave the appearance of an approaching storm—dust came rolling up along with the sounds of the panic-stricken mob, and from down the streets came the sounds of windows being shut and doors being barricaded. There was nothing to be seen on the streets, nothing but people running. I thought that if those Fascist Japanese executioners could witness this moment, they would certainly be content; how proud of themselves they would be . . . they could see for themselves . . . . [51]

The war seemed to be following Hsiao Hung, even though she desperately sought peace and stability, and with Chungking being regularly subjected to bombardment, she once again began to look elsewhere for sanctuary. She and Tuan-mu Hung-liang ultimately made plans to leave Chungking and fly to Hong Kong, and in the spring of 1940 she came to say goodbye to her friends. Most of them were against her decision to leave, but typically she chose not to heed their advice; none of them would ever see her again.

CHAPTER 6

# Hong Kong

### Arrival in Hong Kong: 1940

**D**URING the year and a half Hsiao Hung was to spend in Hong Kong she was constantly torn as never before between her personal and professional needs. Everyone who has written of her life in the British Colony has characterized her as a desperately lonely, frightened, and gravely ill woman who no longer seemed to have any control over her own destiny. In the midst of all this gloom and sadness she produced two major literary works, neither of which mirrors her personal situation as had, for example, most of her writings in Japan.

The peaceful atmosphere Hsiao Hung sought both for her physical well-being as well as for the opportunity to write was to prove as elusive in Hong Kong as it had been in Wuhan and Chungking. She and Tuan-mu Hung-liang were living on Lo tao (Locke Road) in Kowloon,[1] and each time the relatively peaceful atmosphere of the city was shattered by war alerts, she made plans to return to Chungking. On more than one occasion she wrote Mei Lin of her decision, asking him to look for a place for her to live.[2] But the crises always passed before she carried out her plans, and she stayed on. By the end of 1940 her writing efforts had borne fruit; after a lapse of five years she had finished a second novel, *Ma Po-lo*. Then in December she completed her final novel, the evocative reminiscence of her childhood home, *Tales of Hulan River*. The former work, of novelette length, is as untypical of Hsiao Hung as the latter is typical. Both testify to the author's genius as a storyteller.

### I Ma Po-lo

For the reader who has grown accustomed to Hsiao Hung's normal style of writing and choice of subjects, *Ma Po-lo* comes as quite a surprise, for it is, with one exception, like nothing else she wrote before. In a period when humor and satire scarcely existed, this novel is in places exceptionally humorous and framed in heavy satire. That such a work emerged from Hsiao Hung's pen at any time in her career is surprising, and yet it should not come as a total shock, for its origins precede Hong Kong by at least several months. Ma Po-lo, the hero of the novel, is none other than Ho Nan-sheng of "Flight from Danger." His attitudes are similar, his speech is nearly identical (he has not abandoned his favorite phrase, "When the time comes, then what'll we do?" but has supplemented it with yet another: "Those God damned Chinese!"), and though his family situation is different, the main event in his life as we see it—flight from approaching war—not only remains the same but, in this greatly expanded version, has become an obsession. In his flight from the war (which he predicts—almost hopes—will come), from his family, and mainly from reality, Ma Po-lo exposes the hypocrisy of others, though he himself is no less a hypocrite. He is a sometimes raucous, sometimes pathetic, sometimes cunning, and sometimes hapless bundle of paradoxes for whom every place in which he finds himself is the worst of all possible worlds. He detests his father's obsequious reverence for foreigners and foreign products, yet he too remains in awe of both. He derides his wife's love for money, though he is himself a modern-day King Croesus (or would be if he had the money); an outspoken enemy of weakness, he cowers before his wife and his father. In short, he abhors, and is at the same time the embodiment of, hypocrisy.

After *Market Street* this novel is Hsiao Hung's least-discussed and least-known major work. Published by the Ta shih-tai Book Company in 1940, it had undergone a third printing by March, 1943; unlike her other novels, it seems not to have been republished singly by other publishing houses, either in China or in Hong Kong (see note 8). But this cannot be the reason for its neglect at the hands of critics and readers, for it has been available in an anthology of Hsiao Hung's works since 1958. Nonetheless, only three comparatively detailed references to *Ma Po-lo* have been located, all of which predate 1959.[3] The reasons for its neglect in Communist circles are easy to determine; it is viewed as a technical improvement over earlier works but in content and outlook a step backwards, an indication of the author's divorce from the realities of war and from concern for the people.[4] We shall momentarily note the causes of such a reaction. The lack of interest in other circles is less easy to understand; their near-total silence makes even conjecture an impossible task.

In modern Chinese literature humorous satire has not been among the most popular types of fiction. In fact, only one novelist is normally associated with this type of writing—Lao She (Shu Ch'ing-ch'un 1898–1966). For Lao She, who spent many years in England, where he was fascinated by the works of Dickens, it is not surprising that his early works were primarily comic satires. But by the time he was chosen as head of the Chinese Writers' Anti-Aggression Association (1938) he had stopped writing humorous novels, and although there were undoubtedly attempts by other writers at the type of humorous satires that he specialized in during the late 1920's and early 1930's, evidently none were successful enough to warrant much attention.[5]

That Hsiao Hung would attempt to carry on the tradition of Lao She years after his career had moved in another direction, and that she would handle the new form so well in her first attempt, is certainly an enigma. Unlike Lao She, she evidently had little or no contact with foreign novels of this type, and we may assume that Lao She's own works may have served as her models. Again in contrast to Lao She, who wrote his comic novels abroad or in a peaceful academic environment after his return to China in 1930, Hsiao Hung wrote *Ma Po-lo* during the war, at a time when her own health was failing. There is one distinct similarity between the two writers, however, in that both directed their satirical barbs at many of the unsavory aspects of the Chinese character.

The protagonist of Hsiao Hung's novel, Ma Po-Lo,[6] drifts along the perimeter of wartime China, a self-serving and self-deluding, though not self-supporting, maverick from society. A true anti-hero, he has few redeeming qualities as a human being, though his very despicability makes him, if not a model representative of humanity, at least a lively and engaging fictional character. Ma Po-lo, for whom the war exists primarily as a convenience, is a man of little talent and even less honesty and is content to mouth platitudes, air his own numerous grievances real and imagined, flee from difficulties, and bask in his own pessimism. He is to pessimism what Candide is to optimism; Candide's quest for Eldorado is Ma Po-lo's retreat from approaching doom. The story of his changing fortunes takes him from an affluent environment in Tsingtao to a squalid existence in Shanghai, and eventually into the exodus from the war-torn city to the interior.[7] His every move is considered in terms of his basic philosophy: "In all the myriad situations that arise, one has to leave an avenue of escape."[8]

Although Ma Po-lo is the prime object of Hsiao Hung's often biting satire, he is not the only one; his family in Tsingtao, the Chinese citizenry of big cities, sycophants, hangers-on, and other sordid elements of society are paraded in all their seaminess to the condemnation, delight, and occasional astonishment of the reader. After Ma Po-lo and all he stands for, the greatest abuse is heaped upon his father's uncritical and unchecked praise for Westerners, and his Christian beliefs, or more correctly, his self-serving and wholly unchristian interpretation and application of the modish foreign religion. There is, for example, his father's dealings with the family ricksha-puller, a sickly man whom personal tragedy has brought low, and who has been hired as an act of "Christian charity."

> He pulled the ricksha extremely slowly; when he came upon an incline he pulled and tugged as he frothed at the mouth just like a sickly horse. Panting and gasping, he was at the point of collapse, his strength completely gone.
>
> Ma Po-lo's father, sitting in the ricksha, was a bit anxious, but still felt it was worth it:
>
> "If he could run fast, then wouldn't he want a wage as well? The Lord Jesus has said that a man shouldn't take advantage of others." (p. 191)

Then when the poor man collapses under the weight of all this benevolence and seems to be about to breathe his last grateful breath, yet another "Christian" ethic comes to light as Ma Po-lo's father responds to the suggestion that he be carried into the house with the comment that "the Lord Jesus doesn't like to work in cramped quarters." (p. 193) And should anyone doubt that God works in mysterious ways, Ma Po-lo's father, who dotes on his spoiled and nasty grandson—the second of Ma Po-lo's three children[9]—is on hand to set matters straight:

> One day he hit a little girl in the nose, causing a lot of bleeding.
>
> When Yüeh-se came home his nanny told his grandmother that he had split open someone's nose in school.
>
> His grandfather overheard this news and was quite pleased; he said:
>
> "A little boy has to know how to kick and hit. In the future Yüeh-se will certainly rise to officialdom."

That evening the mother of the little girl whose nose had been split open came over to say that her daughter's nose had become infected and a little swollen; she came to discuss the matter with them and check to see if they shouldn't be sending her to a hospital.

When Yüeh-se's grandfather heard this he quickly said:

"No need, no need, there's no need for all that. God can cure all kinds of sicknesses and infirmities."

With that he knelt down before God and with great earnestness said his prayers on behalf of the little girl whose nose had been split open.

His prayers completed, he stood up and asked the girl's mother:

"Are you also a believer in God?"

"No," she answered.

"Ah, no wonder your child's nose bleeds so easily; it all comes from your not believing in God. Calamities come in great numbers to those who don't believe in God."

He then preached to the girl's mother for a long while, after which she left. (pp. 273–74)

If his parents' ostentatious and somewhat unorthodox religious beliefs have failed to win a convert in Ma Po-lo, their toadyism to foreigners has not (although he never admits it). Under normal circumstances the foreigners whom Ma Po-lo both fears and reveres can do no wrong in his eyes; their every action merely underscores the backwardness of "those God damn Chinese." And yet such a position is not static, for when the decorum of a Western establishment hampers his rapid escape from Shanghai, his attitude undergoes a change: "Foreigners are incredible boors. Everything has to be done according to the rules; you can't even cause a little scene!" (p. 237) For nothing must stand in the way of Ma Po-lo's flight from the approaching war. Flight for him is perhaps man's greatest single achievement, at least if it can be done on his terms. And that, of course, is the catch—it cannot always be on his own terms. As Ma Po-lo's money runs out, what was initially a not wholly unpleasant adventure that made certain demands ("What sort of times are these? They are times of fleeing." "In times of fleeing, how can you manage without economy?") turns into a nightmare of deprivation ("How can anyone flee without money?!"). And so the coming war, which for an entire nation was to be an immense tragedy, was to prove his only salvation, for with the imminent fall of Tsingtao his wife would flee, bringing with her enough money to put flight back into its proper perspective. His plans for the war, though carefully thought out, are not always followed by the "inconsiderate" Japanese forces, however, and he is angered over the slowness of their advance.

Unquestionably this aspect of the novel, a casual and humorous (though certainly not approving) approach to at least one element of society's attitudes during the war, is one which has elicited the frowns of Communist critics. Ma Po-lo comes across, with all his shortcomings and detestable attitudes and actions, as a rogue and a schemer but never a blackguard. He is, cast in his role as the major vehicle for satire, not a particularly complex character, but his escapades make him a most memorable one.

In literary terms there is more than just sardonic humor in *Ma Po-lo*; in typical fashion Hsiao Hung often captures brilliantly the sights and sounds of daily life, this time in the city of Shanghai, especially in the International Settlement where she herself spent the better part of two years. In one long passage describing the booths where national lottery tickets are sold, she has re-created the moods and anxieties of those people who pin their hopes on the improbable event of holding the lucky number, come the day of the drawing.

Probably the major flaw in *Ma Po-lo* is the author's tendency occasionally to overdo the humor that she so uncharacteristically brings to the novel. Though surprisingly sophisticated in the main, it sometimes degenerates into burlesque and grows a bit tiresome. One such episode surrounds Ma Po-lo's sendoff on his first visit to Shanghai preparatory to opening a bookstore as his first attempt at self-sufficiency. What begins as a humorous parody on the family prayer session gets rather out of hand as even the servants begin to fall to their knees, tenpin fashion, and farce emerges. Then there is the overworked detail of Ma Po-lo's kicking over his accumulated bottles of soy sauce and the like each time he enters the squalid little room he lives in before running completely out of money. Finally, with somewhat characteristic carelessness, Hsiao Hung tends to leave too many loose ends, especially regarding her characters. In the novel, Little Ch'en, the man who serves Ma Po-lo as clerk in his unsuccessful venture as a bookseller, and later puts him up in his own shabby quarters when he is down and nearly out, simply disappears once Ma Po-lo is reunited with his wife in a Shanghai hotel. Little Ch'en is a colorless character, but he deserves a better fate.

Such blemishes, however, are relatively minor, and *Ma Po-lo* emerges as a successful, humorous, and eminently enjoyable satire on wartime China, and as such quite unique in that era. It is unfortunate that Hsiao Hung was unable to continue Ma Po-lo's travels through China, as was evidently her plan, for the finished product could well have established her as a first-rate satirist. As it is, this novel shows just how far she had come along as a competent and multidimensional writer within a period of only six or seven years. Moreover, she wrote the novel during one of the most emotionally trying periods of her life, but was still able to keep her despondency largely in check.

From what we have seen thus far, there seems to be little justification for the unfavorable reaction *Ma Po-lo* has received from critics in China, for as a satire on obviously reprehensible traits of segments of Chinese society, especially those concerning the protagonist's attitudes toward resistance to the Japanese, it seems to meet at least the minimum standards of wartime literature. There are, however, many aspects of the novel that place it outside the contemporary mold and, in political terms, detract from its usefulness. Certainly the humor throughout most of the novel runs counter to the "accepted" tone. Moreover, there is the undeniable fact that the war barely appears in *Ma Po-lo*, and the strongest attack on the Japanese invaders is the episode in which a Japanese sailor takes advantage of the wife of one of his own countrymen in Tsingtao before the war (a new facet of Ma Po-lo's character is depicted in this scene—that of a voyeur). Even the protagonist, hardly a pillar of the resistance, comes away from his misdeeds none the worse for wear, for with all his faults Ma Po-lo is a character who not only interests us, but one who somehow gains our sympathy; the reader hopes for his good fortune—unlikely as that prospect may seem—irrespective of his personal qualities. In addition, Hsiao Hung has turned her satire on such sacred cows as wartime patriotic literature and the self-righteous attitudes of patriotic writers.

Unfortunately, we can only assume that it is these aspects that have contributed to the novel's generally adverse reception at the hands of critics in China, for almost nothing specific has been written about it. More than anything else, it seems to have been an embarrassment to these critics, having been written by an otherwise "progressive" writer, whose personal and professional conduct were

sufficiently "correct" to keep her in favor. But, political considerations aside, *Ma Po-lo* shows Hsiao Hung to have been not only an
extremely gifted writer, but a multifaceted one as well.

## II   Tales of Hulan River

Up to this point we have seen that, occasional surprises notwithstanding, Hsiao Hung was most often an introspective and
personal writer who was a master at recording scenes from her own
past and bringing to life for her readers the real people and actual
events in her own life. As a result, her most artistic and moving
works are detailed and ingenious re-creations of things as they
happened, viewed through her own subjectivity and imagination.
*Market Street* and "The Family Outsider" are good examples. She is
not merely dealing in autobiography, though that is part of it, for the
author's presence often simply serves to give continuity and a sense
of verisimilitude to her sketches. *Tales of Hulan River*, her final
major work, is a continuation and at the same time the summit of
her achievements in this area. Highly descriptive and extremely
personal, this book, while not in the strictest sense a novel, is both
poetically beautiful in language and absorbing in content. Like
Turgenev's *Sketches From a Hunter's Album, Tales of Hulan River*
(which could just as easily be translated as *Sketches of Hulan River*)[10] was written in an environment far removed in time and place
from its subject; both benefit by the sense of nostalgia which this
distance produces. Both authors have written of the scenic beauty of
their homelands with seemingly unparalleled skill and feeling, and
of the peasants, to which class neither belonged, with great tenderness and perception, while remaining slightly detached. (For
Hsiao Hung, at least, one can also detect a good deal of impatience
and disappointment in the general view.) There, however, the
similarities end. Turgenev's sketches, while occasionally based on
fact, are nonetheless fiction, fiction bathed in heavy irony and
pregnant with a social message. Hsiao Hung, on the other hand, has
most likely embellished the episodes and character portraits in her
novel, although the entire work is unquestionably largely rooted in
fact and is consequently much more closely aligned to personal
reminiscences. Also of interest is the fact that Turgenev used his
sketches to launch his career, while Hsiao Hung's novel capped
hers.

*Tales of Hulan River* was written at a time when most other
Chinese writers were either writing no fiction at all, occupying
themselves solely with wartime journalistic reportage, essays,
dramas, and the like, or were applying the same anti-Japanese
criteria to their stories and novels—work more in the sphere of
propaganda than art. Hsiao Hung, too, had something to say, but
both the message and the form were of her choosing—she was more
concerned with being an artist than a mere propagandist. The result
is a work far superior artistically to nearly everything else written
during the time, although from a political standpoint the novel and
its author have been subjected to rather severe if not opprobrious
criticism by Communist critics. But it has not been universally
censured, for Mao Tun himself wrote a long preface in 1946, one far
more laudatory than Lu Hsün's earlier Preface to *The Field of Life
and Death*. Mao Tun wrote:

> Some readers may not regard *The Hulan River* [sic] as a novel.
>
> They may argue: No single thread runs through the whole book, the
> stories and characters in it are disconnected fragments, the work is not an
> integrated whole.
>
> Others may look upon *The Hulan River* as an autobiography of an un-
> orthodox sort.
>
> To my mind, the fact that it is not an orthodox autobiography is all to the
> good and gives it an added interest.
>
> And we may counter: The main point is not that this work is not a novel in
> the strict sense, but that it has other qualities more "attractive" than those
> to be found in the average novel. It is a narrative poem, a colourful genre
> painting, a haunting song.
>
> Satire is here, and humour. At the start you read with a sense of relax-
> ation; then little by little your heart grows heavier. Still there is beauty,
> slightly morbid perhaps but bound to fascinate you.
>
> You may complain that the work contains not a single positive character.
> Nothing but poor creatures, full of self-pity, yet choosing to be slaves to
> tradition. And the author's attitude to them is perplexing. Flaying them
> ruthlessly, she nevertheless sympathizes with them. She shows us the
> stupidity, obstinacy and sometimes the cruelty of these slaves to tradition,
> yet presents them as by nature good, not given to cheating, hypocrisy, or
> living in idle comfort, but very easily satisfied.[11]

A bit defensive perhaps, but in the main a glowing criticism. Even
his treatment of the central flaw in the work—by Communist
standards—is unusually mild:

If we search for a weakness in the author's outlook, we shall probably find it not in the absence of positive characters but in the impression their nightmare existence makes on readers. If not for their own stupidity and conservatism, and the trouble they bring on themselves, their life has its pleasanter side. We are shown no trace of feudal oppression and exploitation, no trace of the savage invasion of Japanese imperialism. But these must surely have weighed more heavily on the people by the Hulan than their own stupidity and conservatism.[12]

Other Communist critics reverse the priorities by labelling the novel a major step backwards, a literary fiasco, and further indication of the author's almost total separation from the masses and the "struggle," while admitting that technically and rhetorically it is an improvement over earlier works.[13]

Mao Tun's choice of descriptive words is most apt; no better example of the novel as a "narrative poem, a colorful genre painting, a haunting song" appears than Hsiao Hung's masterful depiction of the sunsets in her homeland:

The sunsets in this place are beautiful to behold. There is a local expression here, "fire clouds"; if you say "sunset" no one will understand you, but if you say "fire clouds" even a three-year-old child will point up to the western sky with a shout of delight.

Right after the evening meal the "fire clouds" come. The children's faces all reflect a red glow, while the big white dog turns red, red roosters become gold ones, and black hens become a dark purple. The old man feeding his pigs leans against the base of a wall and chuckles as he sees his two white pigs turn into little golden pigs. He is about to say:

"Mother's!* . . . even you have changed. . . ."

A man out for a refreshing evening stroll walks by him and says:

"Old man, you are sure to live to a ripe old age; your beard is always golden!"

The clouds burn their way in the sky from the west to the east, a glowing red, as though the sky had caught fire.

The variations of the "fire clouds" here are many; one minute they are a glowing red, a moment later they become a clear gold, then half purple-half yellow, and then a blend of gray and white. Grape gray, pear yellow, eggplant purple, all of these colors appear in the sky. All sorts of colors are there, some which words cannot describe and some that you have never seen.

Within the space of five seconds a horse is formed in the sky with its head facing south and its tail facing west; the horse is kneeling, looking as though it is waiting for someone to climb up onto its back before it will stand up.

Nothing much changes within the next second, but two or three seconds later the horse has gotten bigger, its legs have spread out, and its neck has elongated . . . but there is no longer any tail to be seen.

And then, just when the people watching are trying to locate the tail, the horse disappears from sight. . . . (pp. 34–36)

*A vulgar epithet.

As in *The Field of Life and Death*, there is no hero or central figure in *Tales of Hulan River*, a fact, as Mao Tun has pointed out, its detractors use as evidence of its extra-novelistic status. The work is divided into seven chapters, each of which tells its own story or paints a separate picture, but all are connected by a common locale, a common time, and the observations of the child-narrator. Hsiao Hung has skillfully ordered her narrative from chapter to chapter so that there is a constant crescendo and diminuendo effect achieved by the alternation between tragedy and somberness on the one hand and light humor and satire on the other.

The first chapter is a general description of the town of Hulan, its seasons, scenery, and a wide-angle view of its inhabitants and their view of life, superstitions, foibles, miseries, and cruelties. It comprises more than a brilliant nature study—though it is that, too—as it is also a commentary on people, on a way of life, and even on a system that has formed (or malformed) the populace. The second chapter (all are untitled) depicts the major festivals celebrated and their effect on the people. This chapter also contains a long and absorbingly interesting section dealing with the mysterious ways of the local sorceress and the force her exorcist rites have on the local population. In sum, it is a chapter more about ghosts and goblins than about people, more a tale of superstition and fear than the interaction of human beings. The next two chapters are devoted to the author's grandfather and to the compound in which she lived as a child; we have seen several excerpts from both.

Chapter Five is the tragic tale of a mistreated and misunderstood young girl who is the victim of an arranged marriage. It proves to be the author's vehicle for voicing—in unequivocal terms—her feelings concerning the position of women in society. The following chapter, parts of which are based on "The Family Outsider," concerns once again Hsiao Hung's unique relative, Second Uncle Yu. Though Second Uncle Yu is the source of much humor, the lasting impression on the reader is of sympathy and pity. He, like the pathetic women in so much of Hsiao Hung's writing, is a product of an

unsympathetic society, and the memory of this childless, re-
sourceless, pleasureless existence lasts long after the book has been
finished and put aside. The final chapter is about one of the narrator's neighbors, a "poor but honest" miller.

Individually, each of the seven chapters could, with minor alt-
erations, be an independent work. But collectively their effectiveness is markedly enhanced, and the resultant work is certainly
greater artistically than the sum of its parts, for it puts under a
microscope the entire town, and by extension much of early
twentieth-century Chinese rural society in the Northeast. It is at
once enlightening and compellingly moving.

We have mentioned the author's remarkable talent for seemingly
effortless recall; in *Tales of Hulan River* there are countless
examples. There is, for instance, the long and detailed description of
the paper offerings (houses, animals, people, and so on) which are
burned for the dead and thus are so important to the townspeople.
When the reader reflects on the vividly beautiful and uncannily
intricate products of the craftsmen who devote their lives to such
endeavors while themselves living in an abysmal squalor, he
suddenly experiences a feeling of emptiness over the senseless
burden the purchase of such objects places on the living. In fact, the
almost masochistic manner in which the peasants themselves block
any opportunity to better their own lives comes under severe attack
throughout the novel; like the author herself, the peasants appear as
their own worst enemies. The most scathing attack is the episode
dealing with the child-bride, in which the author excoriates the
peasant attitude of viewing those very qualities usually considered
to be assets—courage, self-confidence, beauty, and health—as
arrogance, and therefore generally undesirable, and brings into
focus the plight of women generally. The latter aspect occasionally
arouses the author to shrill commentary, but usually—and more
effectively—her message is clothed in caustic sarcasm:

The young women, bewildered, cannot understand why they must suffer
such a fate [prearranged marriage], and so tragedy is often the result; some
jump down wells, others hang themselves.

An old saying goes: "A battlefield is no place for a woman."

Actually, that's not true; those wells are terribly deep, and if you casually
ask a man whether or not he would dare to jump down one, I'm afraid the
answer would be "no." But a young woman, on the other hand, would
certainly do so. An appearance on a battlefield doesn't necessarily end in

death, and in fact might even lead to an official position later. But jumping down a well, there's not much chance of emerging alive—most never do.

Then why is it that no words of praise for the courage of women who jump down wells are written into the chronicles of chaste women? They have all been removed by the chroniclers of chaste women, because they are nearly all men, each of whom has a wife at home. They are afraid that if they write such tales, then one day when they beat their own wives, they too may jump down a well; if they did they would leave behind broods of children, and what would these men do then? So with unanimity they avoid writing such things, and concern themselves only with "the refined, the cultured, and the filial . . . ." (p. 57)

A long list of adjectives could be used to describe the peasants as they appear in *Tales of Hulan River*—cruel, morbidly curious, naïve, well-meaning, cowed, misfortunate, mistreated—and there are telling episodes in support of each. But at the head of the list we must place the words "unchanging" and "shortsighted." This description first emerges in a long, partly dramatic, partly narrative, and partly scenic section early in the novel and is reinforced time and again throughout the book.

Though much too long to quote in its entirety here, the section dealing with Hulan's much-discussed dangerous mudhole is a superb indictment of the peasants' inability or unwillingness to get to the roots of their problems and better their own lives. Although the mudhole, situated in the middle of a well-travelled road, perennially claims animal victims and is often nearly responsible for the deaths of local children, it nevertheless remains there year after year, a topic of conversation but never the object of concerted action by the townspeople. There is a poignantly beautiful episode in which a horse nearly dies in this mudhole; both its plight and the selfless actions by neighboring men to extricate it produce one of Hsiao Hung's most memorable passages. Curious bystanders, timorous and laughable gentry, victim and savior alike, all are touched by the dangers of the mudhole—but no one even considers the possibility of removing the hazard. Rather, after each successful maneuvering to pass it, personal satisfaction and pride supplant the fear that this almost revered but certainly unnecessary obstacle had caused moments before:

After five or six minutes of struggling, the mudhole has been crossed. No one ever comments on the fact that he is by then covered with sweat and hot all over. Then comes the next person, who must prepare himself for a dose of the same medicine. There are few choices available to him—about all he can do is grab hold here and clutch there, till after five or six minutes he too has crossed over. Then once he's on the other side he feels re-vitalized, bursts out laughing, and looks back to the next to cross, saying to him in the midst of his difficult struggle:

"What's the big deal? You can't call yourself a hero unless you've faced a few dangers in your life!" (pp. 10–11)

Does all this mean that no thought was ever given to easing the dangers caused by the mudhole? Not at all:

Once an elderly member of the gentry fell into the mudhole at high water. As soon as he climbed out he said:

"This street is too narrow. When you have to pass by this water hazard there isn't even room to walk. Why don't the two families whose gardens are on either side take down their walls and open a path?"

As he was saying this an old woman sitting in her garden on the other side of the wall chimed in with the comment that the walls couldn't be taken down, but that the best course of action would be to plant some trees; if a row of trees were planted alongside the wall, then when it rained the people could cross over by holding on to the trees.

Some advised taking down walls, and some advised planting trees, but as for filling up the mudhole with dirt, there wasn't a single person who advocated that. (p. 13)

As in her other successful works, the range of material covered, the detail, and the emphasis on seemingly insignificant aspects of life in *Tales of Hulan River* are remarkable indeed. Little justice would be served by taking them out of context here, for their brilliance can only be seen as facets of the whole work, and each contributes to the health of the novel and to the generally somber mood it evokes. But the pessimistic tone which is often apparent does not remain unchecked, for despite the collective slavish conservatism and ignorance of her peasants, Hsiao Hung recognizes and recounts the inherent goodness, courage, and redeemability of the individual, exemplified by the one man who continues to live outside the expectations of his peers, even in the face of tragedy. Harelip Feng, whose story is told in the final chapter, is a simple but courageous miller who suffers countless indignities at the hands of those who do not approve of his way of life. His short-lived marital happiness—his wife dies in giving birth to their second child—is the envy of his neighbors, and its termination produces in them smug delight. Harelip Feng's refusal to be intimidated by them and his determination to face his hardships with courage are the sparks of light which penetrate the pervading darkness.

*Tales of Hulan River* is a unique novel, not for Hsiao Hung, for whom it was essentially a climactic continuation of her other personal reminiscences, but in the broad arena of contemporary Chinese letters. The reader of this autobiographical novel who is looking for positive fictional characters is bound to be disappointed. As Mao Tun writes regarding the people in this work: "Harelip Feng of the mill has [the] most vitality of them all, so much so that we cannot but admire his spirit. And yet we find nothing outstanding about his character, apart from the outstanding tenacity of his will to live, and that is a primitive tenacity."[14] He is essentially correct, though his political blinders do not allow him to do justice to Harelip Feng, nor do they permit a closer look at the unique personality of someone like Second Uncle Yu (after all, characters need not be positive ones, in Mao Tun's interpretation of the word, to be enjoyable ones). But in the final analysis, it is the entire town that is depicted here—it has the leading role.

*Tales of Hulan River*, all things considered, must stand as Hsiao Hung's representative work, and the further away from wartime China, in time and geography, the novel's critics get, the more they are inclined to label it her most artistic one. Perhaps this is the single most significant indication of its greatness.

### III  *1941–1942: Illness and Death Under Japanese Occupation*

In the spring of 1941 Agnes Smedley called on Hsiao Hung, whom she had not seen in more than four years. She was alarmed by her physical condition and the tiny, wretched room in which she was living.[15] She immediately took Hsiao Hung to her own residence to stay and urged her to leave Hong Kong.[16] Mao Tun, who was also in Hong Kong at that time, later recalled the events of those few months:

In April . . . Hsiao Hung was urged by Agnes Smedley to go to Singapore . . . . Hsiao Hung tried to persuade my wife and me to go too. But I did not want to leave Hongkong, and had work to keep me there. Imagining Hsiao Hung was afraid of being caught in Hongkong when it fell (if war actually broke out there), I did my best to reassure her. Little did I know that her eagerness to leave arose from her sense of loneliness in Hongkong, and that she hoped by leaving Hongkong to escape from that fearful loneliness.[17]

Although not explicit in this passage, the implication is that she was again asking for help; Mao Tun couldn't provide it. Several years of marginal living, the war, and one emotional crisis after another had taken an irreversible toll on Hsiao Hung, and there was no longer any doubt that, in addition to her other ailments, she had contracted tuberculosis. And once again this young woman who had joined her fortunes with a series of selfish and insensitive men was aided in her distress by a woman, as she had been at each previous juncture by Hsü Kuang-p'ing, Ting Ling, Ikeda Yukiko, and Midorigawa Eiko. This time Agnes Smedley arranged to have her admitted to Queen Mary's Hospital on Hong Kong Island and kept her supplied with clothing and money.[18] Evidently, she had hopes of taking advantage of Smedley's benevolence on an out-patient basis, relying on injections and a formidable array of medicines, but she was much too ill by then.

Once in the hospital, her condition and mood improved at first, but that soon changed; having caught a chill, her illness flared up once again, this time even more severely. She needed attention badly, but, due to her obvious poverty, this was not forthcoming. It was to be a repetition of her hospitalization nearly a decade earlier in Harbin, something of which she was obviously aware.[19] She was by then desperate, avoided by her friends and neglected by hospital personnel. No longer able to tolerate staying in the hospital, she contacted Tuan-mu Hung-liang, who was editing the magazine *Shih-tai wen-hsüeh* for Chou Ching-wen, the Hong Kong leader of the Northeastern China People's Movement (Tung-pei ti min-tsu yün-tung), asking him to have her released. He and Chou came to see her and advised her to stay. Another door had closed in her face. She then tried to leave on her own, but was stopped by the hospital staff—Chou had by then offered to pay her hospital bills for up to six months. Finally she found a friend willing to intercede on her behalf, Yü Yi-fu, a member of the Northeastern Salvation Association (Tung-pei chiu-wang hsieh-hui), and with his help left the hospital and returned to her home, probably toward the end of summer. She was by then so weakened by her illness that she could not move

about on her own and spent most of her time in bed. While re-
cuperating at home she made two new and important friends, the
poet Liu Ya-tzu,[20] whom she first met at her home when he came to
call on Tuan-mu Hung-liang,[21] and another Northeastern writer,
who later became her biographer, Lo Pin-chi.[22] Lo had come to
Hong Kong from Kweilin to find a position, and after he was unsuccessful with Mao Tun, he turned, successfully, to Tuan-mu
Hung-liang.[23]

For Hsiao Hung, the situation remained static over the next few
months, the only item of importance being the completion of a long
short story, "Hsiao ch'eng san-yüeh" (Spring in a Small Town), her
last piece of creative writing. This story has been favorably received
by critics and is one of the few pieces that have been translated into
English.[24] It is the story of a young girl, a relative of the narrator
(perhaps also of the author), who falls in love with one young man,
but is betrothed to another. An amiable, sincere, self-denying, and
clever girl, she nevertheless dies of a broken heart rather than fight
tradition. There are some touching episodes and one or two typically lyrical scenic descriptions, though it is not among Hsiao
Hung's best works.

On December 8, 1941, the Japanese invasion of Hong Kong
began. At nine o'clock in the morning Liu Ya-tzu rushed over to
Hsiao Hung's home, at a time when battles were being fought
throughout the city. Tuan-mu Hung-liang and Lo Pin-chi were
there with Hsiao Hung, who was terrified by the sounds of airplanes
overhead, an understandable fear considering her experiences in
Chungking slightly more than two years earlier, though according to
Lo, what she feared most was being left alone. Her own serious
illness, the warfare and bloodshed all around her, and the realization that she would probably not be able to write the things she had
planned produced in her feelings of helplessness, anger, and regret:

"Leaving Hsiao Chün was the resolution of one problem, and going with
'T' [Tuan-mu Hung-liang] was the beginning of another . . . .

"I should have left 'T' long ago, but I still didn't want to return to my
home. Now I want to surrender to my father, accept my bitter defeat, and
throw away my weapons, because my body has failed me; I never thought I
would see this day.

" 'T' is planning to break out with the others, and after today he won't be
coming back; he's already said goodbye to me. Didn't I already make myself
clear? I want to go back to the puppet state of Manchukuo, and it's your

duty ['C'—Lo Pin-chi] to get me to Shanghai. . . . One day, after I've regained my health, I'll come back. I still have my sequel to *Tales of Hulan River* to write. . . ."[25]

On Christmas day, 1941, Hong Kong fell to the Japanese. Two days earlier Hsiao Hung evidently had suffered a relapse, and she reentered the hospital.[26] On January 13, 1942, she underwent what proved to be an unnecessary operation for a suspected throat tumor at the Yang-ho Racetrack Hospital on Hong Kong Island. After the operation she began to realize that she would not recover this time, and her reaction was a mixture of resignation and an occasional outburst of frustrated anger:

"There were some things I wanted to write, but now I know I'm going to leave you all . . . .Why are you so sad? We all have to die sometime, don't we? The day comes for every one of us; do you imagine you'll live to the age of eighty? The life I've lived has brought my body to this point. Death, what difference does it make? I'm at peace with myself."
She consoled "C": "Don't cry, but go and live a good life . . . I'm not happy about having to leave all of you either!"
Hsiao Hung's eyes were filling with tears as she said in a subdued voice: "But to die like this . . . my heart is heavy . . . ."
"T" stood by her bedside weeping.[27]

At noon on the eighteenth Tuan-mu Hung-liang and Lo Pin-chi accompanied Hsiao Hung in an ambulance as she was transferred from the Racetrack Hospital back to Queen Mary's. At 2:00 P.M. another operation was performed to replace a breathing tube in her throat. She no longer could speak but, with pen and paper, carried on conversations with Lo Pin-chi, who stayed with her around the clock. She spent much of her time consoling her distraught friends, making a big show of her appetite as evidence that she was improving. By the morning of the twenty-first, infection had set in around the incision in her throat, though there was no one who could help—all the foreign doctors had been interned in Japanese concentration camps, and many others, including the sisters, had fled or been taken away. That evening Lo Pin-chi left Tuan-mu Hung-liang with her in the hospital and returned to Kowloon. At dawn on the twenty-second, he returned with an armload of food, only to find Japanese sentries in front of the hospital door and a new sign above it which read "Great Japanese Army Battlefield Hospital." All the patients had been removed. At 9:00 A.M., Tuan-mu Hung-liang met Lo Pin-chi and accompanied him to a provisional hospital set up in a local schoolyard by the Red Cross, telling him that Hsiao Hung had slipped into a coma at six o'clock that morning.

At 11:00 A.M. on January 22, 1942, Hsiao Hung died of a throat infection and other complications arising from advanced pulmonary tuberculosis and other debilitating illnesses. She was thirty years old. The tragedy of death at such a young age and the loss to Chinese letters of a writer of such great potential are further heightened by the irony of her dying under Japanese occupation almost nine years after fleeing from Japanese-occupied Manchuria.

## IV  *Epilogue*

On the twenty-fourth of January, Hsiao Hung's remains were cremated in the Japanese facilities behind the racetrack on Hong Kong Island, and on the following day she was buried in a simple grave near the Lido Gardens (Li-tu hua-yüan) beside Repulse Bay.[28] A wooden marker with the four handwritten characters "Hsiao Hung chih mu" (Hsiao Hung's grave), possibly written by Tuan-mu Hung-liang, was placed in the center of a ring of stones around the grave.[29]

Hsiao Hung's death affected her friends and the writing community in general as no other since Lu Hsün's five years earlier. The news filtered slowly back to her friends in the interior, usually by word-of-mouth. It reached Yenan in early April, and a brief announcement appeared in the *Liberation Daily* on the eighth of April.[30] On the first of May, a memorial meeting was held in Yenan; it was chaired by Ting Ling and attended by many of Hsiao Hung's friends. Among the fifty or so present were Hsiao Chün, Shu Ch'ün, Lo Feng, and Pai Lang; speeches were made by Ting Ling, Hsiao Chün, Shu Ch'ün, and others.[31] There was, in addition , a memorial meeting in Chungking,[32] and although one was planned in Kweilin, it was postponed in light of indications that one of Hsiao Hung's friends was hoping to put such a gathering to his own advantage.[33] It can only have been one of the two men who were with her when she died.

After burying Hsiao Hung, Lo Pin-chi and Tuan-mu Hung-liang went to Kweilin where they stayed with Sun Ling until their unseemly conduct forced him to ask them to leave. The problem surfaced as Sun witnessed a fistfight between the two (Lo won), following which Lo produced a bitter letter written by Hsiao Hung to Tuan-mu Hung-liang accusing him of abandoning her, and a note she had given Lo during one of their muted conversations in which she wrote "I hate Tuan-mu!"[34] Then came the bombshell: Lo had elicited from Hsiao Hung an expression of love for him, after which he had promised to marry her when she recovered her health. But being a cautious man, he carefully recorded her instructions regarding the copyrights on her writings; they were: *Market Street* was to go to her younger brother, *The Field of Life and Death* to Hsiao Chün, and *Tales of Hulan River* to him. Tuan-mu Hung-liang received nothing.[35] The pair submitted their claims to the Kweilin branch office of the Shanghai Magazine Company, Lo won, and the issue was closed. The whole incident was certainly a seamy epilogue to Hsiao Hung's life and only strengthens the conviction that a major aspect of her personal tragedy was an unending victimization at the hands of men. The pity of her deathbed statement, "The greatest source of sorrow and pain to me was my being a woman,"[36] is that it rings so true.

CHAPTER 7

# *Hsiao Hung and Her Craft*

### I  *Themes and Attitudes*

IN broad terms the major themes in Hsiao Hung's writings can be
divided into two categories: in nonfiction she is autobiographical;
in fiction she writes mainly of the peasants. In the former category
*Market Street* is representative, and even her long reminiscence of
Lu Hsün is highly autobiographical, telling us nearly as much about
the author as about her subject. Among her essays the reader will
search in vain for philosophical treatises, works on literary theory,
or propagandistic writings; she evidently had neither the interest
nor the intellectual breadth to write of such things. Missing, too, are
the self-revelations that would shed light on her literary motivations
and writing habits and methods. Perhaps she herself was unaware of
any influences working on her, the process by which she came to
her inspirations and subjects, and other aspects of her literary
achievements. Generally speaking, she was not especially adept in
nonfiction, nor was she particularly prolific in this area. *Market
Street*, of course, is the major exception, and few if any of her other
nonfiction writings approach it in technical skill and readability.

### 1. *Peasant Characters*

It is primarily in the field of fiction that Hsiao Hung has left her
mark on contemporary Chinese letters, and she has done so on the
strength of but three novels, two of which are considerably shorter
than was generally the rule in fiction of this period. On the basis of
two of these novels, and to a lesser extent, a handful of short stories,
she established herself as one of the foremost portrayers of peasant
life in Northeast China. That is not to say that she wrote only of the
Northeastern Chinese peasants, for such is not the case. We have,
in fact, seen that one of her novels, *Ma Po-lo*, and the short story on
which it was based, "Flight from Danger," were successful pieces of

fiction in which the setting is a major city and the protagonist an urban rather than a rural figure. There are also other themes and other settings, from the teacher in Japan in "The Red Orchard" to the boatman in "The Yellow River" to the little boy speaking at the revolutionary school in "The Child's Speech." But it is still the peasants whose stories are told in most of her successful pieces of fiction. Her attitude toward the peasants is usually a mixture of compassion and affection with an observable dose of displeasure and chastisement. She is drawn to them by the oppression they have traditionally suffered at the hands of rapacious landlords, greedy townspeople, warlord armies, outside invaders, and capricious natural forces. For her, they are both pathetic and courageous, mistreated and doggedly stoic; but they are seldom wise, and are all too often the perpetuators of their own misery.

Lacking the conviction of a Communist, for whom party leadership is the only alternative to the status quo, she sees the peasants themselves as their only true hope for betterment, and therefore praises their innate potential while castigating them for their unimaginative conservatism. She was neither a socialist nor a Marxist, but a humanist and individualist by conviction. She thus condemns the senseless cruelty and lack of compassion on the part of the peasants, for besides offending her sensibilities, such actions and attitudes she views as self-defeating. The chapter in *Tales of Hulan River* dealing with the abominably cruel treatment of the child-bride is one of her strongest indictments anywhere. That a blameless human being (especially a woman) should suffer the physical and mental abuses the girl receives is sheer anathema to her and appears as a recurring theme in much of her fiction, taking on the form of an obsession.

Harelip Feng is another victim of this cruel treatment (as is his common-law wife, who receives much the same type of treatment as the child-bride), but he either has the strength to rise above it or is blissfully ignorant of its intent. In an attack on the sort of deadening morbid curiosity that brings out countless numbers of spectators to executions and other public demonstrations of man's inhumanity to man, she exposes yet another weakness of her peasants:

Someone spotted a coil of rope on Harelip Feng's brick bed [k'ang] and quickly spread the rumor that Harelip Feng was planning to hang himself.

Talk of a "hanging" proved a powerful stimulant. Women fastened on their scarves, men put on their felt boots; those who were coming to watch the fun or who were making plans to come, it's hard to tell just how many there were.

There were more than thirty people, not counting the children, in Old Yang's family in the West Compound. With the children that made over forty. . . . Figuring that among them there were some who were too old or too sick to come, let's say that only ten of them turned out. So that makes ten from Old Yang's family in the West Compound, and three from Old Chou's family in the same compound. . . .

Then there were quite a few of the men—how many exactly it was hard to tell—who made bean noodles, stoked the furnace, or ran errands for the mill. At all events, not less than twenty or thirty from our compound went to watch the fun. They were joined by innumerable others from the neighborhood who came as soon as the word reached them.

A hanging! Why should a good man choose not to live but prefer to hang himself? Hurry up and see! This is something too good to miss! Hurry up and see!

Besides, it doesn't hurt to look. After all, it isn't like a circus where you have to pay admission.

That's why crowds always gather when a woman in the town of Hulan River jumps down a well or into the river, or when a man hangs himself. I don't know if this is true all over China, but at least it applies where I come from.

A woman who throws herself into the river is not buried as soon as they recover her body. Her corpse is left on the bank for a couple of days for everyone to see.

A woman who jumps down a well is not buried as soon as they recover her body, but displayed to the curious eyes of eager spectators just like an exhibition of native products.

And yet these are not pleasant sights. If Harelip Feng had hanged himself, he would have been a gruesome sight.

Timid women cannot sleep for several nights after seeing the body of a suicide. But the next time some unfortunate takes his own life, they flock around just the same. The fearful and vivid impression they take home makes them lose their sleep and appetite again, but as if under some strange compulsion, they go a third time, even though it frightens them nearly out of their wits. They buy yellow paper money and a bundle of incense sticks to burn at the crossroads, then kowtow three times towards the north, south, east, and west, imploring the evil spirits:

"Don't take possession of me! I've sent you off with incense and paper money!"

One girl died of fright after seeing a hanged corpse. And I heard of another who died of fright after seeing a body brought up from a well. She fell ill from the shock and no doctors were able to save her.

Yet people choose to look, and men, perhaps because they are bolder, are not afraid. Most women are more timid, but they screw up their courage to go.

Women even take their children along to look. Long before they've even grown up they're taken along, perhaps to accustom them to this exciting world of ours, so that they will not be totally inexperienced in the area of suicides.[1]

Such characterizations appear fairly often in Hsiao Hung's depictions of peasant life, peasant attitudes, and peasant values (with or without the sardonic tone), and show that she has not idealized the peasantry as have so many other authors, including the prolific nineteenth century French novelist, George Sand, with whom Hsiao Hung has been compared.[2] Her approach is a more honest one. For her the daily struggle of the peasants for a reasonable livelihood is not so much a burning issue as it is a fact of life, a story which needs telling. Having told their story in two novels and several short stories, Hsiao Hung established herself as the foremost chronicler of rural life in Northeast China in the early 1900's.

## 2. Feminism

In the course of this study regular mention has been made of Hsiao Hung's frequent outbursts against men. In point of fact, the theme of feminism is highly visible in all her major works except *Ma Po-lo*, a satire in which the hero is a male. It is not surprising that such commentary should pervade nearly all her works, since on a personal level she was a constant victim of male arrogance and mistreatment and of a social system in which men viewed women as playthings, alter egos, supporters, servants—everything but equals. Hsiao Hung's anti-male attitude manifests itself in two forms in her writings: specific, isolated, and often strident outbursts, and the less direct, often more effective method of making most of her major characters women—usually pathetic ones—and leading the reader through a step-by-step revelation of their debased position in a male-dominated society. For example, Wu-yün Sao in "On the Oxcart," has been the victim of her husband's inability to weigh his actions in the context of his family; in "At the Foot of the Mountain," the crippled woman and her daughter have been abandoned by her man; and the women are badgered in several of the sketches in *The Bridge*. Additionally, many of the chapters in *The Field of Life and Death* and *Tales of Hulan River* powerfully depict the sufferings of women at the hands of men; and finally, Ts'ui-yi, the heroine of

"Spring in a Small Town," is driven to her death by a social system which denies the rights of choice and happiness to its women. But on the assumption that her message has somehow escaped her reader, Hsiao Hung has, from her earliest writings through *Tales of Hulan River*, regularly punctuated both her fiction and nonfiction with occasionally ironic, often angry, and sometimes extremely eloquent indictments of man's inhumanity to woman. There is a bit of all three—irony, anger, and eloquence—in the following excerpt from *Tales of Hulan River* regarding the idols in the two major temples in the town, the Temple of the Patriarch and the Temple of the Immortal Matron:

The people who cast the clay idols were men, and they fashioned the female figures with a gentle appearance, as though out of respect to women. They fashioned the male figures with a savage, malignant appearance, as though in condemnation of men's dispositions. That, however, is not the case. Throughout the world, no matter how fiercely savage, there has probably never been even one man who had flaming eyes. Take Westerners, for instance; though their eyes are different than those of Chinese, the difference is simply that theirs are a limpid blue, somewhat resembling those of cats, and by no means are they flaming. The race of people with flaming eyes has never appeared on the face of the earth. Then why have the people who cast the clay idols made them look that way? For the simple reason that a single glance will strike fear into someone, and not only will he kowtow, but he will do so with absolute conviction. Upon completing his kowtows, when he rises and takes another look, there will never be the slightest regret; the thought that he has just prostrated himself before an ordinary or unremarkable individual would simply not occur to him. And why have the makers of idols cast the female figures with such appearances? That is in order to tell everyone that gentleness indicates a trusting nature, and that the trusting are easily taken advantage of; they are telling everyone to hurry and take advantage of them.

If someone is trusting, not only do members of the opposite sex take advantage of them, but even members of the same sex show no compassion.

To illustrate, when a girl goes to worship at the Temple of the Immortal Matron, all she does is ask for some sons and grandsons. Her prayers ended, she rises and leaves, and no manifestations of respect are apparent. She has the feeling that the Matron of Sons and Grandsons is nothing but a common, ordinary woman who just happens to have a surplus of children.

Then when men hit their wives they can say:

"The Immortal Matron is supposed to be in constant fear of being beaten by the Patriarch, so what makes a gossipy old woman like you any different?"

So it is obvious that for a man to beat a woman is a Heaven-ordained right, blessed by the gods and demons alike. No wonder the figure in the Temple of the Immortal Matron has such a gentle look about her—that comes from having been beaten so often. It becomes evident that gentleness is not the exceptionally fine natural disposition it has been thought to be, but rather the result of being beaten, or perhaps an invitation to receive a beating.[3]

This passage clearly shows that Hsiao Hung brought a good deal of intellect, reasoned judgment, and rhetorical skill to her arguments.

In another, more heavily ironic, passage the author exposes the hypocrisy of one of Hsiao Chün's friends vis-à-vis prostitutes; it is but one of several references to the sexual attitudes of men toward women:

"Those women are really pitiable; some are completely drained of any color, but there they still stand, pulling in customers. . . ." He often went with money in his pocket to take pity on those women.
"No people live more wretched lives than those women, but no one really knows much about them." This he said with the airs of a scholar. Once said, he climbed onto a streetcar, took his money with him, and in all earnestness betook himself to those women to do some research in the "social sciences."[4]

As a general rule Hsiao Hung avoids the topic of sex in her writings or treats it with great reserve. There is one exception: the encounter between the young girl Chin-chih and her lover in *The Field of Life and Death* is graphically described and is filled with animal imagery; it has been excised in all but the earliest edition.

### 3. Anti-Japanese Writings

Resistance to the Japanese is often cited as a dominant theme in the writings of Hsiao Hung. The proponents of this view have apparently confused theme with setting, however; the war (which, after all, was being fought against the Japanese throughout most of her career) was the setting for two of her three novels—allowing the final third of *The Field of Life and Death* to represent the entire novel—and the majority of the author's short stories and prose sketches written after 1937. But the theme in nearly every case is to be found elsewhere; the war itself is usually incidental and functions primarily as a backdrop. It would be wrong, of course, to intimate that Hsiao Hung wrote nothing that could be called "anti-Japanese literature" or that she was not one of the originators of this type of writing. Nonetheless, this aspect of her writing has been vastly overemphasized; while it should properly be viewed as the genesis of her career, in literary terms it is not a salient feature of her *oeuvre*. It is more than a little ironic that as her talents as a writer increased, her reputation in the eyes of many critics diminished, to the point that she is often remembered only as an anti-Japanese writer, and that reputation is often made to rest on her weakest and least skillful novel, *The Field of Life and Death*, a novel that was seriously impaired by its forced anti-Japanese ending.

## II  *Literary Style and Techniques*

In any discussion of Hsiao Hung's style, first mention should be made of her effortless and simple, though often poetic, language. With the exception of almost the entirety of *Tales of Hulan River* and a few of the more spectacularly beautiful passages in other writings, this quality may be overlooked on a first reading, primarily because her language is so natural and flowing; but it is at the very core of her success. Her prose is unaffected, almost never convoluted or overly intricate, and distinctively feminine. This does not mean that it lacks power, since forceful language need not be bombastic, nor should a simple prose style be equated with a juvenile lack of sophistication. For language to be effective it must fit the scene, the situation, and the characters who employ it. Given her choice of settings, motifs, and characters, she has wisely refrained from using turgid, overblown, or inappropriately intricate language, both in dialogue and descriptive passages. Even when her characters lack depth due to an absence of believable emotion or adequate development, they still speak naturally and convincingly, and often on that basis alone nearly come to life.

We have had occasion to note in preceding pages Hsiao Hung's remarkable ability to record the incidental scenes and objects which bring the larger picture into sharper focus and lend naturalness and honesty to her works; it is often these detailed descriptions of seemingly insignificant odds and ends which, more than any other single aspect, create in her writings the desired tone, whether tragic, nostalgic, or sardonically humorous. In a word, the artistry with which she captures for her readers the essence of her people, settings, and events, is what gives her works their sense of realism.

The style of writing that Hsiao Hung customarily employs depends less on characterization, psychological investigation, and prolonged drama than on rhetorical beauty and deep authorial involvement. By temperament an autobiographical and personal writer, there is an almost inverse relationship between her degree of detachment and the success of her works. The greater the element of fiction in her stories, the less convincing they become. Nearly every protagonist in her fiction is a woman, and with one or two exceptions, her female characters are her only successful ones. But besides the sex of her protagonists, there are other notable leitmotifs, among which are the high preponderance of members of the servant class, and the often-repeated situation of a child living with only one parent, or on occasion a grandparent. As for mood, there is no question that most of her writings are tragic and deal primarily with the victimization of defenseless or guileless people. Occasionally, as we have seen, they suffer because of their own attitudes, but more often it is the landed, the rich, and the military—foreign or native—who are the villains in her fiction. In some of her stories the victimization comes about as a sort of cosmic irony, in that fate holds the cruelest punishments for those who least deserve them, people whose very goodness or courage is the source of their vulnerability.

Surprising as it may seem for a writer of her talent and reputation, Hsiao Hung has created but one truly memorable fictional character, Ma Po-lo, and he is a satirical stereotype who undergoes no particular development, nor does he surprise the reader. Unfortunately, this is also true of most of the protagonists in her short stories and in the highly episodic *The Field of Life and Death*. In her shorter works such a phenomenon is of lesser consequence, since by its very nature the short story seldom allows for great depth of characterization. But the lack of a protagonist in her first novel (or for that matter, any character with some real depth) is one of the major factors in its relative lack of success. And so we must conclude that a pervading and important weakness in Hsiao Hung as a writer of fiction has been her inability to produce characters who either convince or surprise. That is not to say that her characters all represent a faceless chorus, for the very ideas that many of them personify are sufficiently engaging or moving to keep them in the reader's mind. Since so much of what she did write was of such high quality, even without the benefit of multidimensional characters, it is tempting to think of what she could have done had she been able to master this aspect of her craft.

Much has been made by some writers of the influence others may have had on Hsiao Hung's works. Mei Lin has written that, " . . . following her separation from Hsiao Chün, with the exception of her retaining a degree of her frank nature, her 'malleability' was readily apparent in every respect; she was easily influenced by those around her, even in her writing style."[5] In the personal sphere, there can be little argument with his statement, although it seems more correct to say that this "malleability" is apparent throughout her adult life. But there is considerably less evidence in support of his contention that her writing style was so easily influenced following her separation from Hsiao Chün.

As we have already seen, *Ma Po-lo*, one of the two major works she wrote after leaving Hsiao Chün, may have been inspired by the early works of Lao She; this novel is certainly like nothing any of her close associates or companions ever wrote and shows no evidence of having been materially influenced by any of them. *Tales of Hulan River*, on the other hand, though typical of Hsiao Hung in theme and style, offers us an opportunity for comparison with a work by another writer—Tuan-mu Hung-liang's *The Great River*. There are several thematic similarities in these two stylistically different novels which were written while Hsiao Hung and Tuan-mu Hung-liang were living together.[6]

We had occasion earlier to note the phenomenon of the unusual sunsets in Hsiao Hung's native home. These "fire clouds," with their brilliant colors and ever-changing shapes, also appear in *The Great River*, but with considerably less effect. Tuan-mu Hung-liang tends to use simile; Hsiao Hung relies on the more evocative metaphor. He treats his subject intellectually; she is more personal and sensual. Then too, her description is an integral part of a broad scenic and sociological canvas, while for him it is but a minor interlude in the course of his narrative. There are other examples, the most obvious being the long episodes in both works involving a sorceress and the rites of exorcism. In *Tales of Hulan River* Hsiao Hung introduces the exorcist theme in an early chapter with her customary descriptive brilliance, then reintroduces her sorceress in the chapter concerning the mistreated child-bride. Tuan-mu Hung-liang's account, which is also of considerable length, is similar to Hsiao Hung's in specialized terminology, but again his highly academic narrative lacks the evocative appeal of the one in *Tales of Hulan River*. His detachment in these and other instances is as evident as her involvement. Hsiao Hung's descriptions are much more satisfying, as her detailed scrutiny of her subjects gives them a vibrant richness which Tuan-mu Hung-liang's cannot match.

That borrowing was involved here cannot be questioned. But by whom? Whatever the relevance of this question, a definitive answer is most likely not forthcoming. Nonetheless, the superior effects produced by Hsiao Hung's handling of each of the themes suggests that if they did not originate with her, they certainly should have. It seems likely, therefore, that whatever the degree of influence others had on her personally, in her writing she continued to take her own counsel and relied not on the ideas of others, but on her own natural inclinations and talent.

Looking at the entire corpus of Hsiao Hung's writings, which by one estimate totals in excess of 700,000 words,[7] the works on which her reputation and position as an important modern Chinese author must be based are *The Field of Life and Death* (for its historical impact, if not its literary qualities), *Market Street, Ma Po-lo, Tales of Hulan River*, and two or three short stories. The qualities of these works that make them the successes they are have already been discussed at sufficient length for our purposes, though to be fully appreciated they must, of course, be read in their entirety and in the original. We must conclude that Hsiao Hung's true genius (for in the terms we have put forth, it can be considered nothing less) lay in her ability to re-create the scenes in her own past and depict the lives of the Northeastern Chinese peasants and the natural beauty of their land with great feeling, perception, and clarity. Hers was the talent of the artist[8] who chose words as her medium of expression; her creations, at their best, remain highly moving and absorbing works of art.

Unfortunately for Hsiao Hung, as for other writers of the 1930's and 1940's, whether her works will endure and will continue to be read and enjoyed for years to come depends as much on the dwindling readership as it does on their own literary merits. Generally speaking, literature from this period cannot be read either on the China Mainland or in Taiwan—Hsiao Hung's are no exception. Translation is but a temporary and extremely limited solution,[9] though as in the case of dissident writers from many nations and periods, it may be the only means of acquiring a readership for some time to come. For the moment, however, only in Hong Kong, and perhaps in a few Chinese communities throughout the world, is there any prospective readership for Hsiao Hung's works; beyond this there are the relatively small academic circles in a few nations in which her and other authors' works are being studied. Considering the impact of literature on the political and sociological developments in modern China, as well as the intrinsic literary worth of much of what was written during the period, we can only hope that the coming decades will witness renewed interest in the literature of Republican China and the men and women who created it.

# Conclusion

HSIAO Hung's life fell just a few years short of spanning the tormented period from the 1911 Revolution to the founding of the People's Republic, an era of almost constant warfare. Absorbingly interesting as the story of her short life may be, it was perhaps more typical in many respects than may seem evident in this isolated study. Her life was largely formed and limited by the political situation in China, and her death was largely a result of it. Looking back on her adult life, we can see that she was certainly outside the traditional mode of women, though her life style seems to have been shaped more by a series of mainly unfortunate events, the perilous age in which she lived, and the people surrounding her than by any natural rebelliousness or inner strength.

There were undeniable attractions in the new order where women were, in theory at least, on a relatively equal footing with men. In the major urban areas the young population was looking for new models; Hsiao Hung probably typified a large segment of this population for whom modernity was to be achieved at almost any price, but who were all too often ill-equipped physically and emotionally to handle the new life style. For women the trials and changes were especially difficult, and only the strongest were able to emerge relatively unscarred. But Hsiao Hung was not a strong woman. Raised in the environment of a conservative family and made to feel largely unwanted, she began her adult life at a distinct psychological disadvantage, compounded by her own sensitive nature and unworldliness. Had this been the sole extent of her problems she could still have looked forward to a reasonably stable and uncomplicated life; but, as we have seen, there were at least two other forces which were to make such an ideal unattainable, one external and one internal. During her twentieth year the initial phase of war with Japan began in her own backyard, as it were, and

129

she was to spend the remaining years of her life trying to keep ahead of it. In less than eight years she travelled many thousands of miles, never staying in one place for more than two years, usually considerably less. After being forced to leave Harbin, she was driven by approaching war from Shanghai, Lin-fen, Sian, Wuhan, and Chungking, only to flee ultimately into Hong Kong and the beginning of World War II. This, her final ill-advised choice, is indicative of the tragic inner flaw which was to prove of even greater consequence to her than the war with Japan.

Regarding the other factor, Hsiao Hung's own writings and the recollections of her friends show that she was a woman who yearned for self-reliance, though in retrospect it is evident that she had an overpowering need to be dependent on others, primarily men. Her disinclination to heed the advice of genuinely concerned women friends, while acquiescing to the desires and demands of men points out this particular weakness, which was a major source of her personal tragedy. She seems to have had a knack for placing herself in unnecessarily difficult circumstances and then choosing the least desirable avenue of escape, thereby compounding her grief. One sees in this rather tortured figure an almost masochistic delight in subjugating her own talents and peace of mind in the often degrading and physically taxing service (as scribe, mistress, and housekeeper) of observably cruel men. Described as a woman "richer in feeling than in intellect,"[1] she saw herself as the female image in the Temple of the Immortal Matron whose trusting nature had set her up as a target for importunate and insincere men. Of the several men who must share this burden, Hsiao Chün is perhaps the best of the lot, for if his abuses were often the most spectacular, his motives were evidently purer than the others' (we must keep in mind the relative nature of this discussion, not unlike choosing the lesser of evils). He must have been genuinely surprised when she took the very uncharacteristic step of leaving him, for his inflated ego would have prevented him from seeing his treatment of her as anything other than proper. The key to that treatment, in addition to his volatile nature, is his view of the sexes, one which he himself has recorded in terse and unambiguous terms:

"Darling, is this what there is to life? To be in love, to have a home . . . ."
Whenever she was feeling happy she threw her arms around my neck and forced me to answer some of her unusual questions.
"Um . . . this is what life is!"

..............................................................
"No, life can't be all that simple . . . there does have to be something else, doesn't there?"

"Well, then there's . . . there's love, a home . . . then there's . . . then I guess there should be children . . . ."

"Besides children."

"That's all there is . . . ." I struck a thoughtful pose for a moment, then continued:

"For a woman, that's all that's needed!"

"I'm not talking only about women . . . there is no division in 'life' between men and women . . . ."

"Well then, for a man . . . you have to add one thing—earning a living . . . ."[2]

His terms thus spelled out, he loved her in the only manner he understood. For her it was not enough.

Tuan-mu Hung-liang, on the other hand, made no such claims. For him, she was a well-known and well-placed writer who was to be exploited. Why she continued to stay with him when she realized this is hard to understand, though it does serve to strengthen the argument that she was a desperately lonely woman prepared to sacrifice even her self-respect for a permanent relationship with a man. Hsiao Chün and Tuan-mu Hung-liang were not the only men whose often brutal treatment of Hsiao Hung contributed to her growing frustrations, melancholy, and ineffable anger, but they are the most important. Her inability or unwillingness to break free from unhappy relationships with men caused great consternation among her women friends, who considered this the root of her problem. Midorigawa Eiko has written: "Ikeda [Yukiko], who saw her a great deal of the time in Shanghai, said to me with frustrated anger and great feeling on several occasions, 'Why would a progressive writer like her be so much weaker in her personal life than men, and let herself be so completely under their control?' "[3]

Concurrent with Hsiao Hung's emotional decline and psychological problems was a relentless worsening of her physical health, plagued as she was by a variety of illnesses throughout her productive life. Such a situation affected both her career and her emotional state, as she was often physically unable to continue her writing.

Hsiao Hung was lonely and tormented, though she need not have been, at least to the extent she was, for in her brief nine years on the literary scene, from Harbin to Hong Kong, she was often surrounded by friends, many of them well-known literary and political figures. Her extremely close relationship with Lu Hsün and Hsü Kuang-p'ing and their obvious fondness for her, her friendships with Mao Tun, Hu Feng, and countless other writers, editors, and publishers, plus her short but pleasant association with people like Ts'ao Ching-hua (1896–?), Liu Ya-tzu, Ting Ling, Agnes Smedley, and many others, show that she had a large circle of friends. The spate of eulogies, articles, and commemorative poems that followed her death (none, interestingly, by Tuan-mu Hung-liang or Hsiao Chün[4]), plus the considerable tenderness and grief that pervade most of them, are testimony to the esteem in which she was held by so many.[5]

Interest in Hsiao Hung as a person and a writer continued for years after her death. In July, 1957, her ash remains were located and exhumed. A brief memorial service was held by the Hong Kong literary community on August 3, after which the remains were transferred to China for burial in the city of Canton. This event, which most likely was the motivation for publishing in Peking in December, 1958, *Selected Works of Hsiao Hung*, captured the interest of Hong Kong writers, firing their imagination and sense of nostalgia, and was the source of many writings on her life and works over the ensuing decade and a half.[6]

All of this points to Hsiao Hung's popularity among friends and associates and indicates that in some circles not only has it not been eclipsed by subsequent events, but has increased in spite of them. This is, however, only one indication of her importance as a writer. To determine her position in modern Chinese letters we must look further. First, we must keep in mind that she holds several distinctions: As one of the originators of anti-Japanese fiction, her appearance on the literary scene coincided with the beginning of a pronounced shift in the trend of Chinese literature toward progressively more doctrinaire, propagandistic forms (though, it must be remembered, she did not follow the trend that she had helped put into motion); she was one of a small number of women writers in an age when Chinese literature was largely dominated by men; and she was the only woman writer in Lu Hsün's influential coterie. Though her output was not large by most standards, in retrospect she was probably the most talented and successful active woman writer of fiction during most of her short career. Beyond this, a good case could be made for placing her at or near the top of women fiction writers throughout the Republican era. Remembering Lu Hsün's opinion in 1936 that she showed promise of surpassing Ting Ling as the leading female writer, an opinion based primarily on *The Field of Life and Death*, there is little question that she did so easily with her later works, though Ting Ling remained a more influential figure. Lu Hsün was, of course, limiting himself to leftists, but, generally speaking, it was leftists who dominated the literary scene and who were in the main the best writers of the period. (Obviously it is Hsiao Hung's association with leftists rather than any political activities on her part on which her inclusion in their ranks is based.) Thus she must be considered one of the foremost modern writers of her sex, but we must not stop there, for just as there should be "no division in 'life' between men and women," neither should such an artificial distinction be placed on art.

Hsiao Hung's impact on the leftist writing community was substantial, though largely confined to personal terms; until her arrival in Hong Kong she had published but one novel, *The Field of Life and Death;* the nonfiction account of her life in Harbin with Hsiao Chün, *Market Street;* and an assortment of generally un- distinguished short stories and sketches. During the war—that is, after July, 1937—she was either nonproductive or outside the mainstream of current trends of creative writing, something for which she has incurred the displeasure of many of her friends. She was censured for being misguided and immersed in self-pity and characterized as a writer who had lost direction and had "locked herself up in her own little world."[7] The comment by Liu Wu-kou is representative: "She thought that she was one of the many people in the world struggling against bitterness and misery. But somehow she didn't really belong to the masses; she was separated from the people."[8]

In the view of her friends, physical and emotional torment had alienated her from the realities of life and the mainstream of Chinese society; such a situation, they felt, could only foster the creation of unhealthy literature. In the eyes of many, if not most, of her contemporaries, as well as subsequent literary critics in China, her later contributions neither matched her earlier potential nor met the needs of the age, and her position in modern Chinese letters, her personal appeal notwithstanding, was seriously jeopardized.

Thus in literary histories which have been produced since 1949 she is accorded the rank of a second-rate writer, whose personal life is more an object of discussion than her writings, and who is chided for the "wasted efforts" of her later works as much as she is commended for *The Field of Life and Death* and other sundry early works. According to these literary historians, she cannot be considered in the same category as the "giants" of modern Chinese literature, luminaries such as Pa Chin (Li Fei-kan 1904–    ), Kuo Mo-jo, Lu Hsün, Mao Tun, and Lao She, and they also compare her unfavorably with many lesser-known (and usually less-talented), but highly political writers.

In any comparison with her contemporaries, it is apparent that there is little common ground in terms of subject matter and approach. If we have been correct in our assessments of Hsiao Hung's successes and failures, in literary terms, then we are left with the conclusion that her lasting achievements are in other than traditional forms; that is, of her successful major works, only one is a novel in the purest sense, and that one, *Ma Po-lo*, is a humorous satire. The inescapable conclusion then is that more than anything else she was a most unique writer.

When comparing Hsiao Hung's works with those of the most influential, prolific, and talented novelists of the age—from the humorous novels of Lao She to the broader examinations of society by Mao Tun and the romantic revolutionary novels of Pa Chin—the differences are clearly apparent. To some degree there is a topical and doctrinaire message—whether patriotic, communistic, or anarchistic—at the core of the majority of novels by the latter writers that is generally missing in hers. She has combined her artistic talents and personal view of the world to produce works which are both more personal and more appealing, when removed from the context of the age in which they were written, than those of most of her contemporaries. This tends to give the best of her writings a sense of timelessness and personal appeal, inasmuch as the reader is more intimately involved with the author herself. This involvement can only enhance the attraction her writings have on a readership for whom the chaotic period of the 1930's and 1940's in China is less an emotional involvement than an intellectual one. Consequently, unlike so many novels which mirrored the revolutionary activities of their time and strengthened public participation in them, but whose very contemporary nature carried the seeds of their oblivion, her writings will perhaps prove more durable.

It is, of course, too early to produce a definitive statement regarding Hsiao Hung's ultimate position in twentieth-century Chinese letters (at any rate such a statement would necessarily be in the realm of value-judgment, and entirely subjective), but despite her limited output and the mediocre quality of some of her writings, three, and perhaps more, of her works may well prove to have qualities that will help them to transcend time and space. As the appeal of so much of what was written in Republican China abates in proportion to its distance from the time of its creation, the apparent enduring qualities of Hsiao Hung's best writings may ultimately establish her as one of the foremost literary talents of her time.

# Notes and References

1. Owen Lattimore, *Manchuria: Cradle of Conflict* (New York, 1932), p. 14.

2. Although Hsiao Hung entitled her autobiographical novel *Tales of Hulan River* and refers to the town of her birth as Hulan River throughout the work, maps list it only as Hulan.

3. Hsiao Hung, *Tales of Hulan River* (Hong Kong, 1958), pp. 4–6. For a detailed history of the novel and a discussion of its use as a source of biographical information, see Chapter VI below.

4. Hsiao Hung, "Yung-chiu ti ch'ung-ching ho chui-ch'iu" (Perpetual Longing and Pursuit), *Pao-kao* (Shanghai), inaugural issue (January 10, 1937), p. 73. This autobiographical sketch was written at the request of the American journalist Edgar Snow (1905–1972) and was to be used in his collection of short stories, *Living China: Modern Chinese Short Stories* (London, 1936). Hsiao Hung's stories did not appear in the published collection, however, so neither did the sketch. August 6, 1911 is given as Hsiao Hung's birthdate in Charles K. H. Chen, *A Biographical and Bibliographical Dictionary of Chinese Authors* (Hanover, N. H., 1971), p. 25, the only reference to a precise date located. In communication with this writer, Chen was unable to provide substantiating documentation. Tempting as it is to adopt this date, it must remain suspect until corroborating evidence is unearthed.

5. Ch'iao Yin [Hsiao Hung], "Tun tsai yang-ch'e shang" (Crouching on a Ricksha), *Ch'iao (The Bridge)* (Shanghai, 1936), p. 83. All writings by Hsiao Hung under whatever name will, after the initial entry, subsequently be listed under Hsiao Hung, the name by which she is best known.

6. Hsiao Hung, "Perpetual Longing and Pursuit," pp. 73–74.

7. Hsiao Hung, "Chia-tsu yi-wai ti jen" (The Family Outsider), *Niu-ch'e shang (On the Oxcart)* (Shanghai, 1937), p. 41.

8. Hsiao Hung, *Tales of Hulan River*, p. 87.

9. Lo Pin-chi, *Hsiao Hung hsiao chuan (A Short Biography of Hsiao Hung)* (Shanghai, 1947), p. 4. (Hereinafter referred to as *Biography*.) This

biography originally appeared serially in *Wen-ts'ui*, 6–12 (November, 1946–January, 1947).

10. Ching Sung [Hsü Kuang-p'ing], "Chui-yi Hsiao Hung" (Recollections of Hsiao Hung), *Wen-yi fu-hsing*, I, No. 6 (July 1, 1946), p. 652.

11. Hsiao Hung, *Tales of Hulan River*, p. 87.

12. After Hsiao Hung struck out on her own years later, this brother, whose name is not known, was the only member of the family with whom she had any contact; she met him at least once in Harbin and then again in Shanghai in 1936.

13. Hsiao Hung, *Tales of Hulan River*, p. 75.

14. *Ibid.*, p. 87.

15. *Ibid.*, p. 77.

16. *Ibid.*, p. 98.

17. Hsiao Hung, "The Family Outsider," *On the Oxcart*, p. 85.

18. Hsiao Hung, "Ch'u-tung" (Early Winter), *The Bridge*, p. 97.

19. Hsiao Hung, "Perpetual Longing and Pursuit," p. 74.

### Chapter Two

1. *Biography*, p. 3, gives the date as 1929, but Hsiao Hung herself recalls the occasion of a demonstration while she was a student in 1928 (see below).

2. Lattimore, *Manchuria: Cradle of Conflict*, p. 260.

3. Hsiao Hung, "Yi-t'iao t'ieh-lu ti wan-ch'eng" (The Completion of a Railroad), *Hsiao Hung san-wen (Prose Writings of Hsiao Hung)* (Chungking, 1940), p. 77. All of the information regarding the demonstration is taken from this account.

4. Except where noted, the facts concerning Hsiao Hung's school years given below are taken from the first three chapters of *Biography*.

5. *Biography*, p. 19. Lu Hsün (Chou Shu-jen 1881–1936) was a native of Chekiang Province. For more on him, see Chaps. III and IV. Mao Tun (Shen Yen-ping 1896– ), also from Chekiang, was an accomplished translator and literary critic and one of the most prolific and popular fiction writers of the time. He rose to high position in the People's Republic, eventually becoming Minister of Culture. A victim of the Great Cultural Revolution, he has only recently (1973) resurfaced.

6. *Ibid.*, p. 12. This description seems somewhat hagiographic, as available photographs show her "twinkling" eyes to be on the small side.

7. The earliest account of her relationship with this man is given in Shih Huai-ch'ih, "Lun Hsiao Hung" (On Hsiao Hung), *Shih Huai-ch'ih wen-hsüeh lun-wen chi* (Shanghai, 1945), p. 94, where he is identified as a law student. Lo Pin-chi (*Biography*, p. 23) suggests that Li (for that is what Lo calls him) was a teacher at the school.

8. Sun Ling, "Hsiao Hung ti ts'o-wu hun-yin" (Hsiao Hung's Disastrous Marriages), *Fu-shih hsiao-p'in* (Taipei, 1961), p. 33. The two main sections

of town were Tao-wai and Tao-nei, the latter Chinese, the former primarily Russian.

9. *Biography*, p. 25.

10. Ching Sung, "Recollections of Hsiao Hung," p. 652.

11. Hsiao Hung, "Early Winter," *The Bridge*, p. 95.

12. The following account of Hsiao Hung's life alone in Harbin comes from Sun Ling's writings and his personal recollections conveyed directly to this writer.

13. Although most writers, including Lo Pin-chi (*Biography*, p. 33), contend that the editor was the Northeastern woman writer Pai Lang (Liu Li), the wife of yet another Northeastern writer, Lo Feng (surnamed Chang?), and that she dispatched San Lang (Hsiao Chün) and Hei Jen (Shu Ch'ün) to investigate the matter, I have relied instead on the version given by those who were there and were in a position to know. See, for example, Sun Ling, "Hsiao Hung's Disastrous Marriages," p. 34; and Ch'en Chi-ying, "Sho Gun no omoida" (Remembering Hsiao Chün), *Mondai to kenkyu* (Tokyo), II, Nos. 11–12 (combined) (August-September, 1973), p. 148.

' 14. For documentation of the information which follows, see Ko Hao-wen [Howard Goldblatt] and Cheng Chi-tsung, "Hsiao Chün tzu-chuan chi ch'i-t'a" (Hsiao Chün's Autobiography and Other Facts), in *Chung-hua yüeh-pao (The China Monthly)*, no. 723 (December, 1975), pp. 49–52.

15. The account which follows is based primarily on the writings of Sun Ling and the conversations this writer had with him in January, 1974, in Taipei.

16. Lo Pin-chi, Sun Ling, and virtually everyone who knew Hsiao Chün have written of this trait. Hsiao Hung herself hints at her suspicions of his infidelities in her writings.

17. Tu Chün-mou, "T'ien Chün Hsiao Hung ti hua-chi ku-shih" (The Humorous Story of T'ien Chün and Hsiao Hung), *Tso-chia ni-shih* (Shanghai, 1937), pp. 164–167, offers an interesting scenario by asserting that the reputed enmity which later developed between Shu Ch'ün and Hsiao Chün stems from this episode.

Shu Ch'ün (surnamed Li), a native of either Korea or Tumen, a Chinese city on the Korean border, was a frequent contributor to many periodicals in Shanghai, Wuhan, and Yenan. Never a subject of public attack, he was most likely one of the many writers from the 1930's and 1940's whose careers came to an end during the Great Cultural Revolution in the late 1960's.

18. Ch'en Chi-ying, "Remembering Hsiao Chün," p. 140.

19. Lo Pin-chi, after remarking that Hsiao Hung was pregnant before meeting Hsiao Chün, simply drops the subject. Later (*Biography*, p. 58) he writes that she entered a Harbin hospital in the winter of 1933 to give birth to Hsiao Chün's child, a daughter whom she left in the hospital just prior to leaving Harbin herself. Lo's account is refuted by Sun Ling, who is abso-

lutely certain that at no time during his acquaintanceship with Hsiao Hung in Harbin (from late 1932 until just before her departure a year and a half later) was she pregnant, nor did she spend any time in hospital. Hsiao Chün has written at length of Hsiao Hung's hospitalization; his account ends with the setting up of their first home, which occurred in 1932. See Hsiao Chün, "Wei-le ai ti yüan-ku" (For the Sake of Love), *Shih-yüeh shih-wu-jih (The Fifteenth of October)* (Shanghai, 1937), pp. 119–178.

20. In a letter dated July 16, 1935, Lu Hsün congratulated the couple on the third anniversary of their union. See Hsü Kuang-p'ing, ed., *Lu Hsün shu-chien (The Correspondence of Lu Hsün)* (Hong Kong, 1964), II, p. 819 (hereinafter referred to as *Correspondence*).

21. This is borne out by Hsiao Hung; the final line in the opening chapter of her reminiscences of this period, set in Harbin on her and Hsiao Chün's first day in their hotel room, says: "Dawn was breaking; it was now the second day, the second day since we had been kicked out of a friend's home." See Ch'iao Yin [Hsiao Hung], *Shang-shih chieh (Market Street)* (Shanghai, 1936), p. 7.

22. Hsiao Chün, "Lü-yeh ti ku-shih," (The Story of a Green Leaf), *The Story of a Green Leaf* (Shanghai, 1936), pp. 7–8.

23. Hsiao Hung, *Market Street*, p. 113.

24. Although this collection was sent to Lu Hsün (see below), it was evidently never published again. In an advertisement in a 1947 republication of Hsiao Chün's *Ti-san tai (The Third Generation)* by the Harbin Lu Hsün wen-hua ch'u-pan she (operated by Hsiao Chün), *Trudging* is listed as one of six books awaiting publication. At least one of Hsiao Hung's contributions to *Trudging* is extant. "Yeh-feng" (Night Winds), which she mentions as one of the pieces included (*Market Street*, p. 137), appears in *Hsiao Hung hsüan-chi (Selected Works of Hsiao Hung)* (Peking, 1958), pp. 7–15. Another piece in *Selected Works*, "K'an feng-cheng" (Watching Kites), dated June 9, 1933, may also have been originally included in *Trudging*.

25. Hsiao Chün, *Pa-yüeh ti hsiang-ts'un (Village in August)* (Peking, 1954), Epilogue, p. 1.

26. Hsiao Chün, *The Story of a Green Leaf*, Preface, p. iv.

27. Two of the final chapters in *Market Street* describe a bout with a stomach ailment that forced her to make several trips to a free clinic and eventually spend two weeks at a friend's house. She continued to be bothered by stomach problems for several years; see her "Shih-mien chih yeh" (A Sleepless Night), *Ch'i-yüeh*, No. 1 (October 16, 1937), p. 16.

28. Ching Sung, "Recollections of Hsiao Hung," p. 652.

### Chapter Three

1. Chang Mei-lin, a native of Canton Province, was very active throughout the war years, particularly in the Wuhan-based Chinese Writ-

ers' Anti-Aggression Association. He was purged as a member of the "Hu Feng Clique" in 1955.

2. See Mei Lin, "Yi Hsiao Hung" (In Remembrance of Hsiao Hung), *Mei Lin wen-chi* (Hong Kong, 1955), p. 26.

3. *Ibid.*, pp. 26–27.

4. *Ibid.*, p. 27.

5. *Ibid.*

6. Hsiao Chün does not name the second manuscript sent, calling it simply a small collection of stories that he and Hsiao Hung had written jointly in Harbin. See T'ien Chün [Hsiao Chün], "Jang t'a tzu-chi" (Let Him Speak for Himself), *Tso-chia*, II, No. 2 (November, 1936), p. 345. This article, written as a memorial to Lu Hsün two weeks after his death, is comprised of the first nine letters he had written to Hsiao Hung and Hsiao Chün, with explanatory notes added by the author which do not appear in *Correspondence*. For easy reference, in subsequent notes from this article the corresponding page numbers in *Correspondence* have also been given. The pseudonym T'ien Chün has been dropped in favor of Hsiao Chün.

7. Jen-min wen-hsüeh ch'u-pan she pien-chi pu, ed., *Lu Hsün jih-chi* (*Lu Hsün's Diary*) (Peking, 1959), II, p. 1,012. (Hereinafter referred to as *Diary*.)

8. Mei Lin ("In Remembrance of Hsiao Hung," p. 28) says they kept the paper going until the end of November and boarded the ship in early December. This cannot be accurate. Hsiao Chün, (*Village in August*, Epilogue, p. 1) recalls that they arrived in Shanghai in November. An examination of Lu Hsün's second letter to Hsiao Chün ("Let Him Speak for Himself," pp. 345–346; *Correspondence*, II, pp. 766–767) and *Diary*, II, p. 1,013, shows that they were already in Shanghai by the third of November, and they had been there for several days. Ching Sung ("Recollections of Hsiao Hung," p. 651) states that they arrived in Shanghai in October, as does *Biography*, p. 80, whose source was Ching Sung.

9. Five pieces in *The Bridge* were written in December, 1933, and March, 1934.

10. Hsiao Chün, "Let Him Speak for Himself," p. 346.

11. Mei Lin, "In Remembrance of Hsiao Hung," pp. 29–32, is the primary source for their early days in Shanghai.

12. Hsiao Chün, "Let Him Speak for Himself," pp. 351–352; *Correspondence*, II, p. 771.

13. An excerpt from a letter from Hsiao Hung appended to Hsiao Chün, "Let Him Speak for Himself," p. 363.

14. *Ibid.*, p. 353; *Correspondence*, II, p. 773. Ching Sung ("Recollections of Hsiao Hung," p. 652) mistakenly gives the date of the meeting as the 27th, the day the letter was sent. *Biography*, p. 84, duplicates the error.

15. Hsiao Chün, "Let Him Speak for Himself," p. 356.

16. Harriet Mills, "Lu Hsün: 1927–1936. The Years on the Left" (unpublished doctoral dissertation, Columbia University, 1963). Also valuable for an understanding of Lu Hsün's later years is Tsi-an Hsia's illuminating essay, "Lu Hsün and the Dissolution of the League of Leftist Writers," *The Gate of Darkness*, (Seattle and London, 1968), pp. 101–145.

17. For more on the relationship between Hsiao Hung and Lu Hsün, including the texts of some of her memorial pieces, see Ko Hao-wen [Howard Goldblatt], "T'an Hsiao Hung yü Lu Hsün" (On Hsiao Hung and Lu Hsün) in the May, 1974, issue (#9) of *Dousou* (Hong Kong), pp. 20–27.

18. *Correspondence*, II, p. 781.

19. Nieh Kan-nu, a native of Hupei, was a well-known essayist and critic, and one of Lu Hsün's most active supporters.

Yeh Tzu (Yü Ho-lin 1912–1939), a native of Hunan, was one of the first and most popular young writers to come under Lu Hsün's wing in Shanghai.

20. *Diary*, II, p. 1,021. Hu Feng's real name is variously given as Chang Kuang-jen and Chang Ku-fei. Born in 1904 in Hupei, he was one of Lu Hsün's closest friends and a dialectician of brilliance and conviction. He was purged in a strident campaign in 1955.

21. *Correspondence*, II, p. 782.

22. See *ibid*, II, p. 785.

23. *Ibid*., II, p. 784.

24. *Ibid*., II, p. 790.

25. *Ibid*., II, p. 794.

26. *Diary*, II, p. 1,047.

27. Huang Yüan (Huang Ho-ch'ing) edited the magazine *Yi-wen* in close contact with Lu Hsün. During the war he served in the New Fourth Army; he was eventually linked with Feng Hsüeh-feng and the *Wen-yi pao* campaign, and was purged.

Ts'ao Chü-jen, a well-known literary critic, died in Macao in 1972 at the age of seventy-two.

28. On May 22, he noted in his diary that he had loaned Hsiao Chün thirty *yüan* (*Diary*, II, p. 1,058); there were probably other occasions.

29. *Ibid*., II, p. 1,056.

30. Hsiao Hung, *Hui-yi Lu Hsün hsien-sheng* (*A Remembrance of Lu Hsün hsien-sheng*) (third printing; Shanghai, 1948), gives the date of her first visit as October first (p. 25) and leaves the impression that she went alone. However, *Correspondence* (II, p. 836) and *Diary* (II, pp. 1,077, 1,081) refute this rather convincingly.

31. *Correspondence*, II, p. 837.

32. From this point on through early 1937 she would use both pseudonyms in magazines and books. Ch'iao Yin, translated literally, means "soft moanings"—an apt choice. Just why the couple chose the name Hsiao

is not clear; their choice of second names is easier: Hung and Chün combined in that order mean "Red Army."

33. *Village in August* was clearly banned (in March, 1936) and is listed among the proscribed works in Chang Ching-lu, ed., *Chung-kuo hsien-tai ch'u-pan shih-liao* (Peking, 1954–1959), III, p. 159. In the Epilogue to *Village in August*, Hsiao Chün writes (p. 3) that both works were banned.

34. *Correspondence*, II, p. 839.

35. Wang Yao, *Chung-kuo hsin wen-hsüeh shih-kao* (Shanghai, 1953), I, p. 253.

36. Hsiao Hung, *The Field of Life and Death*, p. 53. This mention of four of the eight distresses (*pa-k'u*) is but one of several Buddhist references and images in the novel. There are throughout the work many passages that are infused with a heavy Buddhist flavor. Even the title has a Buddhist meaning of birth/rebirth and death/redeath (*samsāra*), although in modern colloquial Chinese "life and death" is preferred over "birth and death." The fatalistic attitude of the peasants in the first part of the novel strengthens the Buddhist tone. Subsequent page references from the novel are given in the text (1958 edition).

37. Nanking University Department of Chinese, ed., *Tso-lien shih-ch'i wu-ch'an chieh-chi ko-ming wen-hsüeh* (Nanking, 1960), p. 173. The novel's primary shortcomings, according to this and other Communist sources, are the pessimistic tone and, more importantly, the misguided and nearly heretical view that uprisings can be spontaneous, independent of party leadership.

38. In a letter to Hsiao Hung written just prior to publication, he went even further: "That sentence in the Preface . . . is certainly not complimentary, and what I mean to say is that the characterizations are not very good at all. But since it is a preface, and we must not lose sight of the salability factor, I figured I should hedge a bit." See *Correspondence*, II, p. 838.

39. Hu Feng's Postface appears only in the original Slave Society series edition, from which this excerpt is taken (p. 5).

## Chapter Four

1. Nym Wales, "The Modern Chinese Literary Movement," Appendix A to Snow, *Living China*, p. 348. This exchange took place during a meeting between Lu Hsün and Edgar Snow.

Ting Ling (Chiang Ping-chih 1907– ), a renowned writer who received the Stalin Prize for Literature in 1951, was a longtime member of the Communist Party and the leading literary figure in Yenan in the 1940's. She was purged in 1958 after a protracted power struggle with Chou Yang, who was himself a victim of the Great Cultural Revolution.

Ping Hsin (Hsieh Wan-ying 1902– ), a native of Fukien, wrote sentimental prose and verse which was immensely popular in the 1920's, especially with the young. She is still active in China, where she works on the writing of children's literature.

2. Ching Sung, "Recollections of Hsiao Hung," p. 652.

3. *Ibid.*

4. Agnes Smedley, *Battle Hymn of China* (New York, 1943), p. 524. The author (1894–1950) spent several years in India before coming to China to observe its revolution. She soon became an active sponsor of the League of Leftist Writers and a close friend of many literary and political figures.

5. Fen Chün, "Lu Hsün fang-wen chi" (An Interview with Lu Hsün), Teng T'ai, ed., *Lu Hsün fang-wen chi* (Shanghai, 1939), p. 132.

6. Tsi-an Hsia, "Lu Hsün and the Dissolution of the League of Leftist Writers," p. 116.

7. Hsiao Hung, *A Remembrance of Lu Hsün hsien-sheng*, pp. 5–6. On page 7 she reiterates that she was a daily visitor.

8. Chou Chien-jen (1899– ) was a botanist who held several important political posts after the Communists came to power. As of this writing he is Vice-chairman of the Standing Committee of the Chinese National People's Congress. He and Lu Hsün were very close—he or his wife were almost daily visitors to Lu Hsün's home in Shanghai—unlike Lu Hsün and his other brother, the well-known essayist, Chou Tso-jen (1885–1966), with whom Lu Hsün quarrelled bitterly in 1923.

9. Hsiao Hung, *A Remembrance of Lu Hsün hsien-sheng*, p. 8.

10. Ching Sung, "Recollections of Hsiao Hung," pp. 652–653. Later Hsiao Hung would write to the author that the medicine had worked so well that she had gotten pregnant. The subsequent loss of the infant, which probably contributed to a further worsening of her health, produced guilt feelings in Hsü Kuang-p'ing, who wrote a poem by way of apology:

> "The flame of life smolders beneath the ground;
> Let it erupt,
> And consume this greedy world
> And the cannibals who kill but never see blood.
> Then be reborn among the cinders,
> Even as a single blade of grass;
> Just as long as your spirit remains." (p. 654)

11. See, for example, Nieh Kan-nu, "Tsai Hsi-an" (In Sian), *Ch'en-yin* (Shanghai, 1948), p. 95.

12. There are, in all, forty-one short essay-length chapters in the book, at least eleven of which had been published previously in 1935–1936 in the periodicals *Wen-hsüeh*, *Wen-chi yüeh-k'an*, and *Chung-hsüeh-sheng*. There is a short Afterword by Lang Hua [Hsiao Chün]. Page numbers have been given in the text following excerpted portions.

13. *Correspondence*, II, pp. 946–947.

14. See, for example, Chou Yang, "Hsien chieh-tuan ti wen-hsüeh" (Literature at the Present Stage), Lin Tsung, ed., *Hsien chieh-tuan ti wen-hsüeh lun-chan* (Shanghai, 1936), pp. 76–77; and Hsin Jen, "Lun tang-ch'ien wen-hsüeh ti chu wen-t'i" (A Discussion of the Problems in Literature Today), Teng T'ai, ed., *Lu Hsün fang-wen chi*, p. 99.

15. *Diary*, II, p. 1,126. She had not been to see him for more than a month on this occasion. See *A Remembrance of Lu Hsün hsien-sheng*, pp. 52–53.

16. In a letter to Hsiao Chün written on October 24, she recalls the occasion of going to say good-bye to Lu Hsün three months earlier. See Hsiao Hung, "Hai-wai ti pei-tao" (Mournings from Overseas), *Chung-liu*, I, No. 5 (November 5, 1936), p. 289.

17. *Diary*, II, p. 1,127.

18. Feng Hsüeh-feng, *Hui-yi Lu Hsün (Reminiscences of Lu Hsün)* (Peking, 1953), p. 195.

19. Kaji Wataru (1903– ), a graduate from the Department of Japanese Literature at Tokyo Imperial University, was sent to China as a member of a dramatic troupe. There he met Lu Hsün through Uchiyama Kanzo. He and his wife, Ikeda Yukiko (1910–1973), became close friends of Hsiao Hung and Hsiao Chün during the war. He is presently living in Tokyo.

20. Hsiao Hung, "Lu Hsün hsien-sheng chi (II)" (Recollections of Lu Hsün hsien-sheng (II) ), *Prose Writings of Hsiao Hung*, pp. 73–75.

21. Hsiao Hung, "Tsai Tung-ching" (In Tokyo), *Ch'i-yüeh*, No. 1 (October 16, 1937), p. 29. This piece appears in *Prose Writings of Hsiao Hung* under the title of "Recollections of Lu Hsün hsien-sheng (II)," though in this collection the name of the friend has been deleted.

22. Hsiao Hung, "Ku-tu ti sheng-huo" (A Lonely Life), *On the Oxcart*, p. 96. All excerpts from this volume in this and the following section are noted by page number.

23. The story was originally serialized in the October and November issues of *Tso-chia*. It was evidently the feature piece in the October issue, for a reproduction of the first page of the original manuscript adorns the cover.

24. He had gone to see Lu Hsün on the fourteenth—his memorial piece, "October the Fifteenth," is mistitled (see *Diary*, II, p. 1,139)—bringing with him copies of Hsiao Hung's *Market Street* and one of his own collections of stories.

25. Hsiao Hung, "Mournings from Overseas," p. 289. An editor's note following this short memorial says: "The above is a letter written by Hsiao Hung and sent to her lover, T'ien Chün, after hearing in Japan of the death of Lu Hsün. Because of the great distance, there was no time for us to ask her to write something for this special edition of *Chung-liu*, and we have printed this letter so that the sound of her weeping can blend with the sounds of ours."

26. *Correspondence*, II, p. 1,013.

27. Hsiao Chün, "Let Him Speak for Himself," p. 363.

28. Evidence of Hsiao Hung's emotional state in Japan can be found in a collection of short verses entitled "Sha-li" (Sand Pebbles) which she wrote in Tokyo, ostensibly on January 3, 1937. Published under the pseudonym Ch'iao Yin, these thirty-four verses, some almost *haiku*-like, appeared on pages 164–170 in the inaugural issue (March 20, 1937) of *Wen-ts'ung;* they clearly show her feelings of self-pity and alienation:

> "Friends and enemies, I respect them both equally,
> For both have left their marks on my soul." (#10)

> "When people are lonely
> They don't like to see others who are lonely." (#16)

> "Why isn't there a bell attached to life?
> Otherwise, if you are cast off,
> How can others feel the loss?" (#17)

> "The ideal white horse cannot be ridden;
> The lover in my dreams cannot be loved." (#20)

> "What is the greatest hurt?
> The unutterable hurt is the greatest hurt." (#34)

29. Hsiao Hung, "Mournings from Overseas," p. 289.

30. Hsiao Hung, "Sand Pebbles," p. 166.

### Chapter Five

1. There is considerable conflicting evidence on this score; the estimates of her date of return run from prior to Lu Hsün's death to the fall of 1937. A detailed examination of the available evidence is given in Howard Goldblatt, "A Literary Biography of Hsiao Hung (1911–1942)" (doctoral dissertation, Indiana University, 1974), pp. 151–154.

2. Published in *Ta-kung pao* (Shanghai), April 23, 1937.

3. Kaji Wataru, "Sho Gun to Sho Kō" (Hsiao Chün and Hsiao Hung), *Chūgoku gendai bungaku zenshū geppo*, #8 (September 5, 1962), p. 2. This short newsletter is an insert in Vol. VII of Takeuchi Yoshimi, ed. *Chūgoku no kakumei to bungaku* (Tokyo, 1972).

4. *Ibid.*, p. 3.

5. Sun Ling, "Hsiao Hung's Disastrous Marriages," p. 36.

6. Nieh Kan-nu, "In Sian," p. 90.

7. *Biography*, pp. 99–102.

8. The sketches are of no literary value, though they aid us in certain biographical matters. It should be noted that the possibility exists that other writings have escaped this writer's attention or that some of the undated

pieces in at least one later collection could date from this period, though neither seems likely.

9. See, for example, Ching Sung, "Recollections of Hsiao Hung," p. 654. This episode is the subject of Hsiao Hung's "Chi Lu-ti fu-fu" (Recollections of Mr. and Mrs. Kaji), *Wen-yi chen-ti*, I, No. 2 (May 1, 1938), pp. 33–44; and Hsiao Chün's "Shang-hai san jih chi" (Three Days in Shanghai), *Ch'i-yüeh*, No. 2 (November 1, 1937), pp. 45–51. Kaji personally acknowledged his debt to Hsiao Hung during a conversation with this writer at Tokyo University on April 25, 1974.

10. Hsiao Hung's "A Sleepless Night" is dated August 22 in Shanghai; it is her last dated piece from that city. "The Completion of a Railroad," written in Wuhan, is dated November 27; obviously, she moved to the interior at some time between these dates. *Ch'i-yüeh*, the magazine edited by Hu Feng, published its first issue on October 16, and it is reasonably certain that the members of the "Lu Hsün Faction" were in Wuhan by then.

11. Mei Lin, "In Remembrance of Hsiao Hung," p. 33.

12. Tuan-mu Hung-liang, whose real name is variously given as Ts'ao Ching-p'ing and Ts'ao Chia-ching, was born in 1912 in or near Ch'ang-t'u County, Liaoning. His first novel was published serially in *Wen-hsüeh* in 1937. While Hsiao Hung and Hsiao Chün were in Shanghai, he was at Tsinghua University in Peking, and his early short stories and novels attracted the attention of the reading public. He corresponded with Lu Hsün, his last letter arriving five days before Lu Hsün died—see *Diary*, II, p. 1,139—though he never met him.

13. Mei Lin, "In Remembrance of Hsiao Hung," p. 33.

14. Ch'en Chi-ying, "Remembering Hsiao Chün," p. 141.

15. "K'ang-chan yi-lai ti wen-yi huo-tung tung-t'ai ho chan-wang" (Development and Attitude in the Literature and Arts Movement Since the Beginning of the War of Resistance), *Ch'i-yüeh*, No. 7 (January 16, 1938), p. 195.

16. Ting Ling, *Yi nien (One Year)* (Shanghai, 1939), pp. 41–42.

17. Shih Huai-ch'ih, "On Hsiao Hung," p. 95.

18. Hsiao Chün, *Ts'e-mien (A Side View)* (Hong Kong, 1941), p. 29.

19. *Ibid.*, p. 8.

20. *Ibid.*, p. 15.

21. Nieh Kan-nu, "In Sian," p. 91.

22. *Ibid.*, p. 90.

23. Hsiao Chün, *A Side View*, p. 17.

24. *Ibid.*, p. 26.

25. Ting Ling, *One Year*, p. 138.

26. Nieh Kan-nu, "In Sian," p. 92. The term *ma-p'i* has been translated literally; it is actually a derisive reference to a flatterer. Though less accurate, the more literal translation carries the mood.

27. *Ibid.*, pp. 89–90.

28. *Ibid.*, p. 92. The translation is from the Chinese.

29. *Biography*, p. 116. The statement was made to a certain "C" (Lo Pin-chi dramatically identifies many of the people in his biography with initials only); it becomes obvious later in the book that "C" is the author himself.

30. Nieh Kan-nu, "In Sian," p. 96.

31. Mei Lin, "In Remembrance of Hsiao Hung," p. 34.

32. Hsiao Chün subsequently ran afoul of the Communist Party and was purged in 1948. The best account in English of his tribulations is Merle Goldman, *Literary Dissent in Communist China* (New York, 1971), pp. xii–xiii, and Chapters II, IV, and IX.

33. Ting Ling, *One Year*, p. 113. The play was published in *Ch'i-yüeh*, No. 12 (April 1, 1938), pp. 366–377.

34. *Biography*, p. 126.

35. Mei Lin, "In Remembrance of Hsiao Hung," pp. 34–35.

36. Sun Ling, "Hsiao Hung's Disastrous Marriages," p. 37.

37. The entire episode appears in *Biography*, pp. 130–132.

38. Mei Lin, "In Remembrance of Hsiao Hung," p. 35.

39. Midorigawa Eiko (Hasegawa Teru), an Esperantist, was a good friend of Kuo Mo-jo and became one of Hsiao Hung's close friends in the short time they knew each other. She died in China during the war.

40. *Biography*, p. 134.

41. See, for example, Hsiao Hung, "Ya-fen yi-ping-fa" (Curing Illness with Toothpaste), *Prose Writings of Hsiao Hung*, pp. 85–89.

42. *Biography*, p. 134. Lo Pin-chi does not use the word "draft"; the Epilogue to the novel is dated December 20, 1940, Hong Kong.

43. Sun Ling, "Tuan-mu yung tso fu-hsin-jen" (Tuan-mu Must Always Bear Responsibility), *Fu-shih hsiao-p'in*, p. 183.

44. Chin Yi, "Tao Hsiao Hung ho Man Hung" (Grieving Over Hsiao Hung and Man Hung), *Chin Yi san-wen hsiao-shuo hsüan-chi* (Hong Kong, 1959), p. 148.

45. Though the collection first appeared in May, 1946, three, and most likely all, of the stories were written in Chungking. Two were included in a collection of wartime stories edited by Tuan-mu Hung-liang, *Ta shih-tai ti hsiao ku-shih* (Chungking, 1940); and *Biography* (p. 136) lists one more that dates from this period. The likelihood that they were all written in Chungking rests primarily on their common, albeit generally mild, anti-Japanese tone and on what we know of Hsiao Hung's mood in Chungking. Though only one of the stories could be considered light and humorous, the pessimism and pathos that are evident in the author's scant few writings in the preceding year and a half are much less evident here.

46. Hsiao Hung, *A Remembrance of Lu Hsün hsien-sheng*, pp. 1–2. Subsequent excerpts are followed in the text by the page numbers. The

term *hsien-sheng* normally means "mister." Here, however, it is used with every mention of Lu Hsün's name as a sign of respect. It is also used with the same intent for Lu Hsün's wife. Consequently, it would detract from the author's purpose to use such titles as Mr. Chou, Mr. Lu Hsün, Miss Hsü, etc.

47. The book underwent a second printing in March, 1946, and a third in 1948.

48. In Hong Kong she is reputed to have written a pantomime in honor of him entitled "Min-tsu hun" (The Soul of the People), though I have not seen it. See *Biography*, p. 142.

49. The November 1, 1939, issue (IV, No. 1) of *Wen-yi chen-ti* also included a piece by Hsiao Hung entitled "Lu Hsün hsien-sheng sheng-huo san-chi" (Random Notes on Lu Hsün hsien-sheng's Life); I have been unable to locate a copy of this issue, though it is likely that it is comprised of portions of the larger work.

50. Hsiao Hung, "The Yellow River," in *Wu-hsing-shan hsüeh-ch'ü* (Yenan?, 1940), p. 95.

51. Hsiao Hung, "The Arsonists," *Prose Writings of Hsiao Hung*, pp. 104–105.

### Chapter Six

1. Man Ta, "Tuan-mu Hung-liang mai suan-mei-t'ang" (Tuan-mu Hung-liang Was Selling Sour-Plum Nectar), *Nan-pei chi* (Hong Kong), No. 25 (June 16, 1972), p. 45. The author notes that he met Hsiao Hung at a memorial gathering for Lu Hsün at which she spoke. The time is not given, though October 19, 1940, the fourth anniversary of his death, is a possibility.

2. Mei Lin, "In Remembrance of Hsiao Hung," p. 35.

3. Shih Huai-ch'ih, "On Hsiao Hung," pp. 100–101; Juan Lang, "Ma Po-lo wang ho-ch'u ch'ü?" (Where Has Ma Po-lo Gone?), *Wen-hui pao*, August 3, 1957; and Wang Yao, II, p. 135.

4. Shih Huai-ch'ih, "On Hsiao Hung," p. 101.

5. Mention should also be made of the Hunanese writer, Chang T'ien-yi (1907–     ), who used comic satire in some of his best short stories. See C. T. Hsia, *A History of Modern Chinese Fiction* (2nd ed.; New Haven and London, 1971), pp. 212–236.

6. His original name was Pao-lo (Paul); displeased with having a Christian saint as his namesake, he has adopted the name Po-lo.

7. It is possible that this novel was only the first part of a planned trilogy; it may have been Hsiao Hung's intention to have the hero continue to parallel the author's own travels beyond Wuhan, the point at which *Ma Po-lo* ends.

8. *Selected Works of Hsiao Hung*, p. 163. All subsequent excerpts are from this edition and are identified by page number in the text. In January,

1975, a photo-offset edition of the novel (taken from *Selected Works* with new pagination) was published by the Ch'uang-tso shu-she (Hong Kong).

9. In keeping with the Christian theme, Ma Po-lo's children are all endowed with saintly names: Yüeh-se (Joseph), Ta-wei (David), and Ya-ko (Jacob), the last being his only daughter.

10. There is by no means unanimity in the English title for Turgenev's work, the Russian title of which, *Zapiski okhotnika*, is literally translated as "Notes of a Hunter." The title used here is from Richard Freeborn's 1967 Penguin translation.

11. Mao Tun, "Preface to *The Hulan River*," Chinese Literature (Peking), No. 2, 1963, p. 31. The Chinese original of the Preface can be found in *Mao Tun wen-chi* (Peking, 1961), X, pp. 89–98. The earliest available edition of the novel is a June, 1947, edition by the Huan-hsing Book Company (Shanghai and Wuchang), the one for which Mao Tun wrote his preface. In the biographical sketch which appears in this edition Lo Pin-chi states (p. 4) that the novel was first published in Kweilin, though Hsiao Hung died before seeing a copy. Shih Huai-ch'ih's 1945 article "On Hsiao Hung" (p. 99) gives the publisher of the edition available to him as the Shanghai Magazine Company (see below). In 1954 the Shanghai Wen-yi Publishing Company published an edition for which, it is noted, the 1947 edition was used as a model (within six months this later edition had undergone four printings); in 1958 and again in 1966 the Hong Kong Hsin-yi Publishing Company brought out a photo-copy edition which is the one most readily available today. Excerpted portions in this section are identified by page number from this latest edition.

12. Mao Tun, "Preface to *The Hulan River*," p. 32.

13. See, for example, Shih Huai-ch'ih, "On Hsiao Hung," pp. 101–103; and Fu-tan University Chinese Department, *Chung-kuo hsien-tai wen-hsüeh shih: 1919–1942* (Shanghai, 1958–1959), p. 496.

14. Mao Tun, "Preface to *The Hulan River*," p. 32.

15. *Biography*, p. 142.

16. Smedley, *Battle Hymn of China*, p. 524.

17. Mao Tun, "Preface to *The Hulan River*," pp. 27–28.

18. See Smedley, *Battle Hymn of China*, p. 524; and *Biography*, p. 142.

19. Remembering Hsiao Chün's role in her early hospitalization, she confided to "C" (Lo Pin-chi) that "at the time I thought of Hsiao Chün, and if he had been in Szechuan, I would have sent him a telegram, asking him to come and get me out; he would have come for sure." (*Biography*, p. 146)

20. Liu Ya-tzu (1887–1958), a native of Kiangsu, was a well-known classical poet and an organizer and participant in several poetry societies. A personal friend of Mao Tse-tung's, he became a member of the National People's Congress. His daughter, Liu Wu-kou, was also in Hong Kong at the time, and she too knew Hsiao Hung.

21. Liu Ya-tzu, "Chi Hsiao Hung nü-shih" (Recollections of Miss Hsiao Hung), *Huai-chiu chi* (Shanghai, 1947), p. 45.

22. Lo Pin-chi (1917–  ) was born in Hun-ch'un County, Kirin Province, according to Ichikawa Hiroshi, who has translated Lo's *Hsiao Hung hsiao chuan* into Japanese. See Takeuchi Minoru, ed., *Gendai Chūgoku bungaku* (Tokyo, 1971), XII, p. 452. Lo fled Manchuria after its occupation and came to Shanghai, where he participated in the hostilities following the outbreak of war in 1937. His works were still being published in the early 1960's; he was probably a victim of the Great Cultural Revolution.

23. Sun Ling, "Lo Pin-chi," *Wen-t'an chiao-yu lu* (Kaohsiung, Taiwan, 1955), p. 7.

24. See Bibliography. Published in *Shih-tai wen-hsüeh*, No. 2 (July, 1941), it is included in *Selected Works of Hsiao Hung* and is the title story of a 1961 anthology of Hsiao Hung's stories published in Hong Kong by the Shanghai Book Company. In the biographical sketch in the 1947 edition of *Tales of Hulan River* Lo Pin-chi states (p. 4) that it was written in two nights while Hsiao Hung was bedridden.

25. *Biography*, pp. 151–152.

26. Man Ta, "Tuan-mu Hung-liang Was Selling Sour-Plum Nectar," p. 45. The remainder of this section has been taken exclusively from *Biography*, pp. 154–159.

27. *Biography*, p. 155.

28. *Ibid.*, p. 159.

29. Yeh Ling-feng, "Chi-mo t'an-t'ou shih-wu nien" (Fifteen Years on a Lonely Sandbar), *Wen-yi shih-chi* (Hong Kong), September 1, 1957, p. 20.

30. "Hsiao Hung ping-shih" (Hsiao Hung Dies), *Chieh-fang jih-pao*, April 8, 1942, p. 2.

31. "Yen-an wen-yi-chieh chui-tao nü tso-chia Hsiao Hung" (Yenan Literary Circles Hold Memorial Meeting for Woman Writer Hsiao Hung), *Chieh-fang jih-pao*, May 3, 1942, p. 2.

32. Sun Ling, "Hsiao Chün," *Wen-t'an chiao-yu lu*, p. 4. At this meeting, says Sun, Hsiao Hung's fondness for nice clothes was criticized by her close friend Hu Feng; certainly an unusual eulogy!

33. Mei Lin, "In Remembrance of Hsiao Hung," p. 36.

34. The episode is described in Sun Ling, "Lo Pin-chi," pp. 8–9.

35. *Ibid.*, p. 9. In this article the disposition of *Market Street* and *The Field of Life and Death* is reversed. I have followed the information given in Sun Ling, "Tuan-mu Must Always Bear Responsibility" (p. 184), instead, on assurances from the author that it is correct.

36. Shih Huai-ch'ih, "On Hsiao Hung," p. 95.

### Chapter Seven

1. Hsiao Hung, *Tales of Hulan River*, pp. 236–238.

2. Hsü Ting-ming, "Lun Hsiao Hung chi ch'i tso-p'in" (On Hsiao Hung and Her Works), *Wen-t'an* (Hong Kong), No. 329 (August, 1972), p. 59.

3. Hsiao Hung, *Tales of Hulan River*, pp. 66–67.

4. Hsiao Hung, "Three Bored Men," *The Bridge*, p. 103.

5. Mei Lin, "In Remembrance of Hsiao Hung," p. 35.

6. *The Great River* (Shanghai, 1947) is dated November 25, 1939, about the time Hsiao Hung completed her draft of *Tales of Hulan River.*

7. *Selected Works of Hsiao Hung,* p. 345.

8. It is noteworthy that she never completely put aside her artistic inclinations; the covers of *The Field of Life and Death* and *Ma Po-lo* are both of her design, and during her final months in Hong Kong, according to Lo Pin-chi (*Tales of Hulan River* (1947), Biographical Sketch, p. 4) she did some cover designs and artwork for the magazine Tuan-mu Hung-liang edited.

9. Hsiao Hung has not fared badly at the hands of translators; her works have most often been translated into Japanese, and at least one Russian translation has been found. English translations are given in the Bibliography.

## Conclusion

1. Mao Tun, "Preface to *The Hulan River,*" p. 32. He is paraphrasing a comment by Ching Sung ("Recollections of Hsiao Hung," p. 652).

2. Hsiao Chün, "For the Sake of Love," *October the Fifteenth,* p. 168.

3. Quoted in *Biography,* p. 105.

4. In the Prologue to the 1946 Shanghai edition of *Village in August* Hsaio Chün briefly acknowledges his debt to Hsiao Hung for having copied the manuscript and for subsequently encouraging him to have the book published (p. 3). In the Epilogue to the 1954 edition he expresses his gratitude in a slightly expanded version—one full sentence.

5. A complete listing of those located is included in Goldblatt, "A Literary Biography of Hsiao Hung (1911–1942)," pp. 269–270.

6. Detailed information on the entire episode and events leading up to it can be found in Yeh Ling-feng, "Fifteen Years on a Lonely Sandbar"; Yeh Ling-feng, "Kuan-yü Hsiao Hung nü-shih ti shih-ch'ing" (Some Matters Regarding Miss Hsiao Hung), *Wen-hui pao,* March 9, 1957; Yeh Ling-feng, "Hsiao Hung mu fa-chüeh shih-mo chi" (Notes on the Exhumation of Hsiao Hung's Remains), *Wen-hui pao,* August 3, 1957; Ah Chia, "Hua k'ai shih-chieh yi Hsiao Hung" (Recollections of Hsiao Hung During the Season of Blooming Flowers), *Hsiang-t'u* (Hong Kong), July, 1957, pp. 4–5; and Yeh Te-hsing, "Hsiao Hung ch'ien-tsang shih-liu nien" (Sixteen Years After the Transfer of Hsiao Hung's Remains), *Ming-pao jih-k'an* (Hong Kong), June 16, 1973, p. 7.

7. Shih Huai-ch'ih, "On Hsiao Hung," p. 101.

8. Quoted in *Ibid.,* p. 100.

# Selected Bibliography

Items marked with an asterisk were not available to this writer. In Part I all known editions have been listed.

## I. Works by Hsiao Hung

### 1. Novels

*Sheng-szu ch'ang* (*The Field of Life and Death*). Shanghai. Jung-kuang she, 1935; Hong Kong. Chung-liu ch'u-pan she, 1958.

*Ma Po-lo.* Chungking. Ta shih-tai shu-chü, 1940; Hong Kong. Ch'uang-tso shu-she, 1975.

*Hu-lan-ho chuan* (*Tales of Hulan River*). *Kweilin. Shanghai tsa-chih kung-szu, 1942(?); Shanghai and Wuchang. Huan-hsing shu-tien, 1947; Shanghai. Hsin wen-yi ch'u-pan she, 1954; Hong Kong. Hsin yi ch'u-pan she, 1958.

### 2. Fiction and Nonfiction Collections

**Pa-she* (*Trudging*).

*Shang-shih chieh* (*Market Street*). Shanghai. Wen-hua sheng-huo ch'u-pan she, 1936.

*Ch'iao* (*The Bridge*). Shanghai. Wen-hua sheng-huo ch'u-pan she, 1936.

*Niu-ch'e shang* (*On the Oxcart*). Shanghai. Wen-hua sheng-huo ch'u-pan she, 1937.

*Hui-yi Lu Hsün hsien-sheng* (*A Remembrance of Lu Hsün hsien-sheng*). Shanghai. Sheng-huo shu-tien, 1940.

*Hsiao Hung san-wen* (*Prose Writings of Hsiao Hung*). Chungking. Ta shih-tai shu-chü, 1940.

*K'uang-yeh ti hu-han* (*A Cry in the Wilderness*). Shanghai. Shanghai tsa-chih kung-szu, 1946.

*Hsiao Hung hsüan-chi* (*Selected Works of Hsiao Hung*). Peking. Jen-min wen-hsüeh ch'u-pan she, 1958.

*Hsiao ch'eng san-yüeh* (*Spring in a Small Town*). Hong Kong. Shanghai shu-chü, 1961.

3.  Miscellaneous Writings (by date of publication)

1936

"Ma-fang chih yeh" (A Night in a Stable). *Tso-chia*, I, No. 2 (May, 1936), pp. 475–484.

"Hai-wai ti pei-tao" (Mournings from Overseas). *Chung-liu*, I, No. 5 (November 5, 1936), p. 289.

1937

"Yung-chiu ti ch'ung-ching ho chui-ch'iu" (Perpetual Longing and Pursuit). *Pao-kao*, No. 1 (January 10, 1937), pp. 73–75.

"Sha-li" (Sand Pebbles). *Wen-ts'ung*, I, No. 1 (March 20, 1937), pp. 164–170.

"Pai-mu" (A Visit to a Grave). *Ta-kung pao*, April 23, 1937.

"Shih-mien chih yeh" (A Sleepless Night). *Ch'i-yüeh*, No. 1 (October 16, 1937), p. 16.

"T'ien-k'ung ti tien-chui" (Adornments in the Sky). *Ch'i-yüeh*, No. 1 (October 16, 1937), pp. 17–18.

"Tsai Tung-ching" (In Tokyo). *Ch'i-yüeh*, No. 1 (October 16, 1937), pp. 29–30.

"Huo-hsien wai erh chang" (Away from the Front Lines: Two Essays). *Ch'i-yüeh*, No. 2 (November 1, 1937), pp. 50–51.

"Yi-chiu-erh-chiu-nien ti yü-wei" (Follies of 1929). *Ch'i-yüeh*, No. 5 (December 16, 1937), pp. 135–136.

1938

"*Ta-ti ti nü-erh* yü *Tung-luan shih-tai* tu shu chi" (After Reading *Daughter of Earth* [by Agnes Smedley] and *An Age of Chaos* [?]). *Ch'i-yüeh*, No. 7 (January 16, 1938), pp. 221–222.

*T'u-chi* (*The Blitz*) (3-act play, co-authored with Tuan-mu Hung-liang, Nieh Kan-nu, and Sai K'o). *Ch'i-yüeh*, No. 12 (April 1, 1938), pp. 366–377.

"Chi Lu-ti fu-fu" (Memories of Mr. and Mrs. Kaji). *Wen-yi chen-ti*, I, No. 2 (May 1, 1938), pp. 33–44.

"Fen-ho ti yüan-yüeh" (The Moon over the Fen River). *Ta-kung pao*, September 6, 1938.

1939

"Huang-ho" (The Yellow River). *Wen-yi chen-ti*, II, No. 8 (February 1, 1939).

*"Lu Hsün hsien-sheng sheng-huo san-chi" (Random Notes on Lu Hsün hsien-sheng's Life). *Wen-yi chen-ti*, IV, No. 1 (November 1, 1939).

"Lu Hsün hsien-sheng sheng-huo yi-lüeh" (Brief Recollections of Lu Hsün hsien-sheng's Life). *Wen-hsüeh chi-lin*, No. 2 (December, 1939), pp. 71–78.

### 1940

*"Min-tsu hun" (The Soul of the People) (pantomime).

4. English Translations (by date of publication)

"Hands" (Richard L. Jen). *T'ien Hsia Monthly*, No. 4, 1937, pp. 498–514.

"A Night in a Stable" (Chia Wu and Nym Wales). *Asia Magazine*, September, 1941, pp. 487–489.

"Hands" (Gladys Yang). *Chinese Literature*, No. 8, 1959, pp. 36–52.

"Spring in a Small Town" (Sidney Shapiro). *Chinese Literature*, No. 8, 1961, pp. 59–82.

"Harelip Feng" (Gladys Yang). *Chinese Literature*, No. 2, 1963, pp. 3–24.

## II. Materials on Hsiao Hung

### PRIMARY SOURCES

AH CHIA. "Hua k'ai shih-chieh yi Hsiao Hung" (Recollections of Hsiao Hung During the Season of Blooming Flowers). *Hsiang-t'u* (Hong Kong), July, 1957, pp. 4–5.

CHAO TS'UNG. "Pao-shou nan-hsing ch'i-wu ti Hsiao Hung" (Hsiao Hung, the Perennial Victim of Mistreatment by Men). *Sa-nien-tai wen-t'an tien-chiang lu*. Hong Kong. Chün-jen shu-chü, 1970, pp. 107–112.

CHEN, CHARLES K. H. *A Biographical and Bibliographical Dictionary of Chinese Authors*. Hanover, N. H. Oriental Society, 1971.

CHI LIN. "Hsiao Hung." *Chung-kuo tso-chia chien-ying*. Hong Kong. Wen-hsüeh ch'u-pan she, 1958, pp. 124–131.

CHIN YI. "Tao Hsiao Hung ho Man Hung" (Grieving Over Hsiao Hung and Man Hung). *Chin Yi san-wen hsiao-shuo hsüan-chi*. Hong Kong. Chien-wen shu-chü, 1959, pp. 144–149.

CHING SUNG [HSÜ KUANG-P'ING]. "Chui-yi Hsiao Hung" (Recollections of Hsiao Hung). *Wen-yi fu-hsing*, I, No. 6 (July 1, 1946), pp. 651–655.

HSÜ TING-MING. "Lun Hsiao Hung chi ch'i tso-p'in" (On Hsiao Hung and Her Works). *Wen-t'an* (Hong Kong), No. 329 (August, 1972), pp. 59–64.

KAJI WATARU. "Sho Gun to Sho Kō" (Hsiao Chün and Hsiao Hung). *Chūgoku gendai bungaku zenshū geppo*, No. 8. Tokyo. Heibonsha, September 5, 1962, pp. 1–3.

KO HAO-WEN [HOWARD GOLDBLATT]. "T'an Hsiao Hung yü Lu Hsün." (On Hsiao Hung and Lu Hsün). *Dousou* (Hong Kong), No. 9 (May, 1975), pp. 20–27.

LI HUI-YING. "Hsiao Hung shih-shih san-shih chou-nien" (The Thirtieth

Anniversary of the Death of Hsiao Hung). *Hsing-tao wan-pao* (Hong Kong), January 17, 1972, p. 8.

―――. "Ts'ung Hsiao Hung mu chiang yi-wei p'ing-ti shuo-ch'i" (Talks on the Levelling of the Gravesite of Hsiao Hung). *Li Hui-ying san-wen chi*. Hong Kong. Chung-nan ch'u-pan she, 1961, pp. 63–66.

LIU YA-TZU. "Chi Hsiao Hung nü-shih" (Recollections of Miss Hsiao Hung). *Huai-chiu chi*. Shanghai. Keng-yün ch'u-pan she, 1947, pp. 45–46.

LO PIN-CHI. *Hsiao Hung hsiao chuan* (*A Short Biography of Hsiao Hung*). Shanghai. Chien-wen shu-tien, 1947.

MAO TUN. "*Hu-lan-ho chuan* hsü" (Preface to *Tales of Hulan River*). *Mao Tun wen-chi*. 10 vols. Peking. Jen-min wen-hsüeh ch'u-pan she, 1961, X, pp. 89–98; "Preface to *The Hulan River.*" *Chinese Literature*, No. 2, 1963, pp. 26–32.

MEI LIN. "Yi Hsiao Hung" (In Remembrance of Hsiao Hung). *Mei Lin wen-chi*. Hong Kong. Lison Book Company, 1955, pp. 26–36.

NIEH KAN-NU. "Tsai Hsi-an" (In Sian). *Ch'en-yin*. Shanghai. Wen-hua kung-ying she, 1948, pp. 89–96.

SHIH HUAI-CH'IH. "Lun Hsiao Hung" (On Hsiao Hung). *Shih Huai-ch'ih wen-hsüeh lun-wen chi*. Shanghai. Keng-yün ch'u-pan she, 1945, pp. 92–105.

SHU NIEN. "Hsiao Hung san-pu" (Three Works by Hsiao Hung). *Chung-pao chou-k'an* (Hong Kong), April 10, 17, 24, 1970.

SUN LING. "Hsiao Hung." *Wen-t'an chiao-yu lu*. Kaohsiung, Taiwan. Ta-yeh shu-tien, 1955, pp. 63–67.

―――. "Hsiao Hung ti ts'o-wu hun-yin" (Hsiao Hung's Disastrous Marriages). *Fu-shih hsiao-p'in*. Taipei. Cheng-chung shu-tien, 1961, pp. 33–37.

TATSUMA SYOSUKE. "Sho Kō ni tsuite" (About Hsiao Hung). Takeuchi Yoshimi, ed. *Chūgoku no kakumei to bungaku.* Vol. V: *Kōsenki bungaku(I).* Tokyo. Heibonsha, 1972, pp. 367–375. Originally published as Vol VII of *Chūgoku gendai bungaku zenshū*. Tokyo. Heibonsha, 1962.

TU CHÜN-MOU. "Hsiao Hung yi nu erh tsou Tung-ching: T'ien Chün yü-pei chui-tsung ch'ien-wang" (Hsiao Hung Angered—Off to Tokyo: T'ien Chün Makes Plans to Follow Her Trail). *Tso-chia ni-shih*. Shanghai. Ch'ien-ch'iu ch'u-pan she, 1937, pp. 168–169.

―――. "T'ien Chün chiang fu Jih hui Hsiao Hung" (T'ien Chün About to Travel to Japan to Meet Hsiao Hung). *Tso-chia ni-shih*. Shanghai. Ch'ien-ch'iu ch'u-pan she, 1937, pp. 170–173.

―――. "T'ien Chün Hsiao Hung ti hua-chi ku-shih" (The Humorous Story of T'ien Chün and Hsiao Hung). *Tso-chia ni-shih*. Shanghai. Ch'ien-ch'iu ch'u-pan she, 1937, pp. 163–167.

YEH LING-FENG. "Chi-mo t'an-t'ou shih-wu nien" (Fifteen Years on a Lonely Sandbar). *Wen-yi shih-chi* (Hong Kong), September 1, 1957, pp. 20–21.

————. "Hsiao Hung mu fa-chüeh shih-mo chi" (Notes on the Exhumation of Hsiao Hung's Remains). *Wen-hui pao*, August 3, 1957.

————. "Kuan-yü Hsiao Hung nü-shih ti shih-ch'ing" (Some Matters Regarding Miss Hsiao Hung). *Wen-hui pao*, March 9, 1957.

YEH TE-HSING. "Hsiao Hung ch'ien-tsang shih-liu nien" (Sixteen Years After the Transfer of Hsiao Hung's Remains). *Ming-pao jih-k'an* (Hong Kong), June 16, 1973, p. 7.


· SECONDARY SOURCES

CH'EN CHI-YING. "Sho Gun no omoida" (Remembering Hsiao Chün). *Mondai to kenkyu* (Tokyo), II, Nos. 11–12 (August-September, 1973), pp. 139–149.

FENG HSÜEH-FENG. *Hui-yi Lu Hsün (Reminiscences of Lu Hsün)*. Peking. Jen-min wen-hsüeh ch'u-pan she, 1953.

HSIAO CHÜN. *Lü-yeh ti ku-shih (The Story of a Green Leaf)*. Shanghai. Wen-hua sheng-huo ch'u-pan she, 1936.

————. *Pa-yüeh ti hsiang-ts'un (Village in August)*. Peking. Jen-min wen-hsüeh ch'u-pan she, 1954.

————. *Shih-yüeh shih-wu-jih (October the Fifteenth)*. Shanghai. Wen-hua sheng-huo ch'u-pan she, 1937.

————. *Ts'e-mien (A Side View)*. Hong Kong. Hai-yen shu-tien, 1941.

HSÜ KUANG-P'ING, ed. *Lu Hsün shu-chien (The Correspondence of Lu Hsün)*. 2 vols. Hong Kong. Pai-hsin t'u-shu wen-chü kung-szu, 1964.

JEN-MIN WEN-HSÜEH CH'U-PAN SHE PIEN-CHI PU, ed. *Lu Hsün jih-chi (Lu Hsün's Diary)*. 2 vols. Peking. Jen-min wen-hsüeh ch'u-pan she, 1959.

MAN TA. "Tuan-mu Hung-liang mai suan-mei-t'ang" (Tuan-mu Hung-liang Was Selling Sour-Plum Nectar). *Nan-pei chi* (Hong Kong), No. 25 (June 16, 1972), pp. 44–45.

MILLS, HARRIET. "Lu Hsün 1927–1936: The Years on the Left." Unpublished PhD. dissertation, Columbia University, New York, 1963.

SMEDLEY, AGNES. *Battle Hymn of China*. New York. Alfred A. Knopf, 1943.

SUN LING. "Hsiao Chün." *Wen-t'an chiao-yu lu*. Kaohsiung, Taiwan. Ta-yeh shu-tien, 1955, pp. 1–4.

————. "Hsiao Chün ti pei-chü ming-yün" (Hsiao Chün's Tragic Fate). *Fu-shih hsiao-p'in*. Taipei. Cheng-chung shu-tien, 1961, pp. 28–32.

————. "Lo Pin-chi." *Wen-t'an chiao-yu lu*. Kaohsiung, Taiwan. Ta-yeh shu-tien, 1955, pp. 5–10.

————. "Lo Pin-chi ti t'an-wu lun" (Lo Pin-chi on Graft). *Fu-shih hsiao-p'in*. Taipei. Cheng-chung shu-tien, 1961, pp. 23–28.

————. "Tuan-mu yung tso fu-hsin-jen" (Tuan-mu Must Always Bear Responsibility). *Fu-shih hsiao-p'in*. Taipei. Cheng-chung shu-tien, 1961, pp. 181–185.

T'IEN CHÜN [HSIAO CHÜN]. "Jang t'a tzu-chi" (Let Him Speak for Himself). *Tso-chia*, II, No. 2 (November, 1936), pp. 344–363.

TING LING. *Yi nien (One Year)*. Chungking. Sheng-huo shu-tien, 1939.

WALES, NYM. "The Modern Chinese Literary Movement." Appendix A to SNOW, EDGAR. *Living China: Modern Chinese Short Stories*. London. George G. Harrap & Co., Ltd., 1936, pp. 335–359.

# Index